IS THERE
ANOTHER WAY?

IS THERE ANOTHER WAY?

Words of Wisdom from One of the
World's Great Spiritual Leaders

DADI JANKI

STERLING ETHOS
An imprint of Sterling Publishing Co., Inc.

New York / London
www.sterlingpublishing.com

Library of Congress Cataloging-in-Publication Data

Janki, Dadi, 1916-

Is there another way?: words of wisdom from one of the world's great spiritual leaders/
Dadi Janki.

       p. cm.

ISBN 978-1-4027-6638-1 (alk. paper)

1. Religious life--Brahmakumari. 2. Brahmakumari--Doctrines. I. Title.

BL1274.252.J26 2010

294.5'44--dc22

10 9 8 7 6 5 4 3 2 1

Published by Sterling Publishing Co., Inc.

387 Park Avenue South, New York, NY 10016

© 2010 by Dadi Janki

Distributed in Canada by Sterling Publishing

^{c}/o Canadian Manda Group, 165 Dufferin Street

Toronto, Ontario, Canada M6K 3H6

Distributed in the United Kingdom by GMC Distribution Services

Castle Place, 166 High Street, Lewes, East Sussex, England BN7 1XU

Distributed in Australia by Capricorn Link (Australia) Pty. Ltd.

P.O. Box 704, Windsor, NSW 2756, Australia

Sterling ISBN 978-1-4027-6638-1

For information about custom editions, special sales, premium and
corporate purchases, please contact Sterling Special Sales
Department at 800-805-5489 or specialsales@sterlingpublishing.com.

CONTENTS

INTRODUCTION

Dadi Janki, administrative head of the Brahma Kumaris spiritual centers, travels the world constantly, sharing her inspiration with world leaders, heads of corporations, and ordinary people. Dadi refuses to set limits and boundaries on what is achievable and, in so doing, inspires others to believe that they, too, can make the impossible possible.

In this little book, Dadi provides an opportunity to see your life differently, act differently, and treat others differently. Dadi provides simple, practical guidance on living in a more contented, wise way, and applies her spiritual principles to five key areas of everyday life. Let Dadi enlighten you on being a better you, on improving your relationships, on being happier and more productive at work, on working to create a better world, and on establishing a relationship with God.

PART 1

DADI ON BEING A
BETTER YOU

INTROVERSION

When you have not had any interest in the external world for some time, but instead have only a deep desire to turn inside, this is the sign of the beginning of the journey within. To those who have seen this sign within the self, I say, "Come, I'll show you how to journey within." It's a matter of going within the self, not inside anyone else.

It's hard to break the habit of wanting to know what is happening in other people. It's impossible to know them, so we try to find out about them by talking to a third person. But meditation is only possible when we go inside ourselves. When we go inside, we leave all the external things outside. We have a habit of looking at all the things outside us. Our intellect is pulled toward all those things. Then it becomes trapped by all those things. Sometimes we have the desire to free ourselves, but we just cannot do it. People, habits, possessions all pull us. The world and its atmosphere have a huge influence on us. We have experienced so much uproar and sorrow, and yet it is difficult to let go of the things of the world. This is why many people say that they are searching for spirituality.

When trying to get to know the self and the one up above, we can focus for a little while, but then we get distracted. So, first, we need to cultivate the virtue of introspection—and to understand fully the contrast between introversion and extroversion. When there is extroversion, the mind is pulled outward. As a consequence, the physical senses and the mind race outward and desires arise in the heart. The heart has been deceived in many different ways and so it carries great sorrow. When the mind becomes more introspective, it begins to listen to the heart and then tells the physical senses to quieten.

In order to be introverted, we need to find the time

to be in solitude. You might say that you don't have the time for this, but we all know that if we truly desire something, we are able to find time for it. As you find the time to devote to this deep desire, notice how you also receive everyone's cooperation; others free you to fulfill this desire. So sit in silence in solitude and allow a dialogue to take place between your heart and your mind. The heart may say, "I have never found what I really wanted. When the mind is confused, it won't obey me." But when your mind and heart agree with one another, when they meet in your introversion, you are finally able to see yourself. The mind has stumbled a great deal and so needs rest, so free yourself from all the external things, confusion, and pulls from outside. The heart becomes firm when it doesn't have any desires or attachments. Then, as you sit in solitude, in an introverted way, begin to stabilize your mind by freeing it from the outside world in the same way. When the mind is stable, it brings about a very good feeling and creates great happiness within, happiness that is merged with peace and power.

REFLECTION ON INTROVERSION

I let the body sit quietly; I focus my vision inward and see my heart and my mind. . . .

I observe the feelings in my heart—I see the pain and the yearning and the deepest desire I have to know myself. . . .

I look into my mind, and I see the thousand directions that my mind is pulled—and I bring my thoughts back to focus on my own inner being. . . .

On the screen of my mind, I hold the image of my eternal form of light. I focus on the inner being—the being of light—and in doing so, my thoughts become calmer, more peaceful. I discover that I, the being within, can create the thoughts that I choose. . . .

I create the thought of peace—I hold peace in my mind, and as my mind becomes peaceful, I look at my inner feelings, and in the upheaval, I discover that within my own heart there is a source of love. Within my own inner being is peace and love. . . .

I keep this awareness and hold it—this is who I am . . . a being of light . . . a being of peace. . . . a being of love.

CONTENTMENT

It is part of human honor to be content. In India, the Goddess of Contentment is worshipped and the one who stays content is considered like a god. His hands may be empty, but the heart is content. Some people have everything, and yet, without contentment, it is as if they have nothing—they become like a pitcher without water. What I have to do is to fill my own pitcher (the intellect) with the cool, clear water of contentment and then offer it to others to drink. I need to learn to stay content. To stay content is to be sensible. How do we give others contentment? With a couple of words of love or simply by looking at them with love.

If we are not content, however, we see others as not being content, either, and this makes the soul restless. If we are restless, everything is affected; even the quality of the voice will suffer. If we remain discontent, it becomes a habit always to complain. Someone who is discontent does not like to see other people happy, nor do such people like to help someone who is unhappy.

Those who are content will share their fortune with others. Those who stay content have gratitude and give thanks to God. Such a soul is never jealous. They avoid making anyone dependent on them, but also learn not to be dependant on anyone else. In order to remain content, we need the power of tolerance. We also need God's love. It is God's love that makes the soul clean. When the intellect is clean, our work can be honest. With the power of honesty and cleanliness, we can achieve a great deal. With honesty and good wishes and pure feelings for all, the soul can reach the highest destination and leave the past behind. This is not a matter of superficial contentment, but a very deep contentment.

When the soul is honest, God gives blessings. When there are blessings, the tasks we do will be successful. Contentment follows. Contentment brings happiness, health, and spiritual wealth, and those who are content bestow blessings on others, well-wishers. Incognito donation is the highest form of charity. There is no need to talk about how much you have done or given. In fact, where did everything come from anyway? It is God who has given us divine wisdom and divine insight. Contentment makes the face sparkle. Contented souls are like God—they have everything and need nothing. Such a soul will dance in happiness.

Once I find contentment, my experience will be that my heart is honest, my head is cool, my vision sweet, and my nature easygoing. I will still use the same ears, mouth, and eyes, but my attitude and my heart will have changed. That inner beauty will then be visible from my eyes and through my eyes.

This is not something I am going to do alone. The power that is created in the atmosphere when we all do this together brings forth vibrations of contentment that reach far and wide.

REFLECTION ON CONTENTMENT

Turning inward, I find myself filled with gratitude. . . .
God has given me all the treasures that He has—treasures
of love, of wisdom, of peace, and of joy. . . .
As I feel these treasures filling my soul, I give thanks to
God and am filled with contentment. . . .
From the Ocean of God, all these treasures come to the soul,
and the waves reach not only me, the soul, but they also
reach out into the world. . . .
God's love awakens human hearts and fills them with
joy—God's peace catches human hearts and fulfills all
desires. . . .
God fills each one and each one realizes that this is what it
had been thirsting for. . . .
Filled with these treasures, there is nothing more that I
need. I have not only enough for myself, but the treasures
overflow and reach out into the world. . . .
I am content with my fortune—content in my relation-
ship with God—and content in my relationship with the
world. . . .
These vibrations of contentment restore harmony and calm
to the world—from God, the Ocean of all treasures, waves
of treasures surround each one of us.

HEAD, HAND, AND HEART

Love has a connection with the heart—when we speak about love, we always put our hand on the heart. We don't put our hand on our head, do we? When the hand goes quite naturally to the heart, it reminds us to make sure, before taking any action, that we have love for ourselves from the heart, and then love for everyone else will follow. If I first feel love for myself, then I will be able to perform good actions with my hands.

But if there are complications in your head, what will be the condition of your heart? If there are bad feelings and negativity for others in your vision, what will be the condition of your heart? One type of soul hurts someone else's heart, and the other type of soul helps to heal others' hearts—let each of us check which type of soul we are.

For example, if I steal something with this hand, then I am aware of it with my head and I know and understand that this is what I am doing. My heart also has that feeling. So who am I deceiving? Who am I causing sorrow? If I use the same hand to give a donation, then I can experience happiness within my heart. I am not taking from anyone; I am giving as much as I can.

This is why to keep the head and heart in good condition internally, it is very important to make sure that the mind and intellect are in a good state. The mind can easily become mischievous and run away. It can easily become attracted to something— it thinks, "This is very good; this is very nice; I want it"—and so the hand takes it. In the same way, the desires of the heart do not allow the mind to stay content, so the mind is always stumbling aimlessly.

When I talk about the head and the heart, I am thinking about the physical body and feelings. The head and the heart belong to the physical body. But when I talk about the mind and the intellect, I go deep within myself. When I subtly go deep within, I tell my mind to stay peaceful and I tell my intellect to think in the right way.

In the external world, lots of things attract us, but we fluctuate when we are attracted to those things. On one side there is the attraction of desires for this and that—and on the other side there is a feeling of being weary and tired of the things of the world.

Each one of us should look within ourselves and think about our own selves rather than looking or thinking about others. Habitually we tend to see and listen to external things—what others are doing. Now give yourself time to see yourself and understand yourself.

REFLECTION ON HEAD, HAND, AND HEART

Turning inward, it is time to "see" myself and check myself properly. . . .

I place my hand on my heart and ask my mind honestly, "Mind, where are you stumbling? From whom are you seeking love? To whom are you giving love? Why are you giving that love to them?" . . .

Now I turn my thoughts toward my conscience. I use my conscience in a subtle way to ask my mind and intellect, "Hey mind and intellect, what are you up to?" . . .

I check within: "Am I giving love to somebody to become happy or am I giving love out of attachment?" . . .

I think about attachment; is it making me sad? When I give and take sorrow, I am unable to receive blessings— and unable to give blessings to others. . . .

I check within.

HAPPINESS

When I have one of my many spiritual chit-chats with people, somebody always asks, "What are the virtues that bring happiness? Is it easy or difficult to be happy these days? What kind of happiness brings peace?" If you were to tour around India, Australia, or Europe—indeed, any part of the world—would there be happiness? Or if you were to visit all the different shopping centers in the country, would you be able to buy happiness? If you went to the cinema or the seaside, would you feel permanent happiness? See if you can find happiness somewhere in the world. Even if you go away on a pilgrimage, do you experience happiness as a result?

Happiness comes from within. We need a lot of power to be happy, and it's not easy in today's world to remain positive and cheerful. The things that you think bring happiness are there for a moment, and the next moment they are gone. *We live in a world of impermanence.* We work so hard to claim a position and to earn money, but do they remain with us?

True happiness comes by first knowing and understanding yourself, then knowing who God is, and finally having that same friendship with everyone— through that, you can find real happiness. We are all members of one family, and it is not just a matter of knowing this as a fact; we have to understand this as an experience, and then the happiness of the experience comes to us in a very natural way, and brings power with it. Power comes when we end the weaknesses that lie within us. As I speak, think about what I am saying and experience it. Then you will see for yourself whether it is true or not.

REFLECTION ON HAPPINESS

In silence, I give myself time and space. . . .
When I focus clearly on God and experience the intense love
He gives, then I know internally that everything in my
life and in my "drama" will be fine. I feel the conviction
internally that everything about me (internally) and my
life (externally) will get sorted out. Then my faith in God
really starts to develop. . . .
My life's purpose is to be able to stay peaceful. To be able to
always remain smiling and cheerful . . . let me be such a
human being that every single person in the world identifies
with me and feels that I am their brother or sister.

HUMILITY

In India, when we meet others, we greet them by putting our hands together and bowing—it is a sign of humility. When our hands come together in unity and humility, the hands also give blessings. Humility is a sign of an enlightened soul—a yogi soul.

If I were to talk for an hour on the value of humility, it wouldn't be enough—if you had ten hours, I could talk to you about humility, and still it wouldn't be enough—because humility is the mother of peace and happiness. In our lives, our real mother is humility. Of course, God is my Mother and Father, but humility, I stress, is my mother, too. Humility also gives birth to all the other virtues, so she, too, is a mother. She has the power to chase away all the weaknesses and defects; humility, the mother, has that much strength! So humility itself is a power and has power. A mother gives birth to a child and then sustains and sees that the child grows up to have a good future. So think about it; if humility were your mother and that mother gave you birth and sustained you and brought light into your life, then that light could do much to help others. It's possible, isn't it? Do you think that humility can be described as the mother? Do you believe that humility is the mother who gives birth to all virtues and sustains your life? My humility can help me to have a relationship with God. With it comes safety, too. Why do people feel insecure or lack a sense of belonging? Why do they feel lonely? Is it because of a lack of humility? Not to have humility is a bit like being an orphan.

All children have the same three requirements: They need a home, money, and parents. Without this, a human being is of no use. Imagine the condition of a child without a mother or a father. What would their state be like? They would feel that something is missing in life. If somebody is homeless, we feel sorry for him. If somebody doesn't have wealth, again, we feel pity. But when we receive a good education and sustenance from an early age, we can look forward to a good future ahead. Humility, like a good parent, sustains us so that all virtues can belong to us. With humility, we are able to look within and find a sweet home inside. If we lacked humility, there would be a lot of disturbance within the heart and mind and conflict within the self. We would be fighting with ourselves in different ways—think of the internal state jealousy and animosity create. It is like being hopeless, homeless, and penniless.

We should aim to experience good fortune simply in being the instrument for a task. What else would I want? If I say I need a bed and don't have a bed, at least I have the ground on which to sleep. Even a little sparrow will feed its chicks, so don't you think we would be fed somehow? In India, there is a custom of feeding grains to the pigeons, and I have seen people in the West also feeding the birds. I have seen what love people have for pigeons. So if I am like a pigeon and keep listening to what God is saying to me and I say, "Hee, hee," then surely He will look after me and feed me, too!

REFLECTION ON HUMILITY

For a couple of minutes, I go within. . . .
In that silence, I experience my own humility—I see it as my mother and father. Humility is my protection and my protector. . . .
Inside me, I find that sweet home furnished with the wealth of all virtues. . . .
Here, within the sweet home, I can give thanks to God. . . .
Humility creates so much strength in my soul that I can make that one Supreme Father, the Supreme Soul, belong to me—I feel that that He is mine. . . .
No matter how impure or sinful I may have become, He is the One who uplifts me and then by teaching me to perform elevated actions, He also purifies me.

SELF-HEALING

When we sit in silence and begin to know ourselves, we see that we carry with us many, many things from the past. The mind has been a slave to so much, and the heart has been wounded. We have done wrong and so we have a feeling of guilt; there are doubts in the mind and pain in the heart. You might enjoy the peace of sitting in silence, but what are you going to do with all this other stuff?

When we are physically ill, we look for the cause. Is it because of food poisoning or something in your diet? Is the pollution of the atmosphere or the climate affecting you, or is it because you haven't been able to give the body sufficient rest? When we look at the condition of the mind, we should look at the same things: What have you been feeding the mind? Have you been giving it negative things to think about? Is that the cause of the pain? Or does the pain derive from negative things, or pollution, in the atmosphere around you? It's almost certain that you have not learned how to let the mind rest, and so it loses its peace and becomes restless and tired. When we look inside, we see worry, hopelessness, and fear—and though you may often have tried to overcome them, you probably have not been successful.

Okay, well at least now you understand that these are the causes of mental pain. Now you have to protect yourself from that pollution by giving the mind open space, keeping the heart clean, paying attention, and feeding the mind good, nourishing thoughts. Rest is especially important for the self. Medicine works when we first give ourselves rest. Once we remove the inner tiredness, we can enjoy the fruit.

At one point, I was looking after someone who rejected all the food I was offering. We went to the doctor, who prescribed some glucose, and within half an hour the patient's appetite had returned and she started eating. The reason for the rejection of nutrition was a deep tiredness. Similarly, when the human heart has been without love for a long time, it rejects everything and becomes full of dislike and fear. But when the heart starts receiving real love— pure love—then there is power. In order to heal yourself, learn to love yourself. Do not cause yourself sorrow. Do not criticize yourself. Do not cause yourself pain. No matter what the causes of your distress, forget them. If it is a question of forgiving others, don't repeat the old hurt in your mind. The more you go over it, the more those events and words live in your mind. It's like pouring salt on wounds, bringing yet more pain. Instead, with patience and tolerance, fill yourself with love.

We need a few essential vitamins to nourish the heart back to full health after we have removed the immense tiredness. What is vitamin A? *Atma,* knowing that you are a soul; vitamin B is the nourishment of Baba, or the Father; C confirms that you are his child; vitamin D stands for the drama of the world; vitamin E shows that you are a very special child of the Father—he looked for you and he found you, healing everything. Now we understand that that wound would not heal from a lack of vitamins. Now you understand that you can give yourself the healing love you need at any time. If you need rest, go into silence for a second and your face will begin to sparkle again. If you need nourishment, give yourself some of these spiritual vitamins.

Pay such attention to yourself that the old illnesses of the mind and the heart go away and you can maintain good health and keep the mind, heart, and body healthy. If something even slightly impure and negative comes into your mind or any bad feeling enters your heart, deal with it immediately. Science has been able to create many inventions and finds many cures to illnesses, but they involve the support of other people. This cure means being able to heal the self with silence.

REFLECTIONS ON SELF-HEALING

I give myself time and space. . . .

I let the external rubbish fall away, and I look for the original beauty of my own inner being. . . .

In silence, I discover the original, pure, loving being that I am. . . .

Seeing my own original purity, I begin to love myself. I value and respect myself. . . .

I hold this vision of my original pure state of being. Acknowledging and honoring this, I also accept the mistakes I have made and the weaknesses that I have had. . . .

Now, with courage and determination for transformation, I let go of the things of the past. . . .

As I allow them to dissolve and fade away, I can forgive myself—I am able to have mercy for myself. I forgive . . . I let go . . . and I can forget. . . .

As I do this, the scars and the wounds that I carry begin to heal and the silence becomes sweet—a silence filled with joy. . . .

I have started on a journey of becoming whole, of filling myself with contentment, so that the empty spaces that

caused fear and anxiety previously are filled and there is
no more space for negativity. . . .

In my original state, I was pure—I let this knowledge
emerge. I keep it and watch guard over it so that nothing
can touch this beauty and purity again. . . .

I hold love in my heart for this original pure state of
being—and I resolve to use it in my life.

THE EGO

Nobody is an enemy to anyone else; our biggest enemy is the ego. The ego and truth are opposites—truth is visible through the humility we have, and ego does not allow us to reveal the truth.

Even if you only have a little bit of ego, it will seem enormous—people will comment on it. Think about colored clothes—you don't know if there are any stains on the fabric because of the colors. But when you wear white clothes, you can see even the slightest stain. When we are not on a spiritual path, it is like wearing colorful clothes: We don't even know or realize that we have so much ego. But when you start along a spiritual path, a little bit of ego becomes all too visible.

In our thoughts, our words, our actions, and relationships, there must be purity, truth, and humility—then there is no ego, and then there will be divinity, too. Ego means holding your head high. Humility means holding it neither high nor low. Humility doesn't mean bowing your head down; it means maintaining stability. Not to bow down physically but to say okay, maybe I am wrong and you are right—that is humility. To be an embodiment of humility is to be truthful within and humble, expressing humility in the way you interact with people. This inner humility allows our inner divinity to emerge.

If I have ego, I think I have to teach everyone. If I have humility, I have instead deep feelings, pure intentions, and the desire to learn. Think about this: If someone has the intention to teach, what tone of voice does she adopt? And if somebody wants to learn, what is his tone of voice like? When the ego is stubborn and we try to prove ourselves right, it causes loss of respect. When there is truth, I don't need to prove it.

Neither do I have to say you are wrong or cause sorrow to another—everything will work itself out. When there is truth within me and purity and cleanliness in my thoughts, then there is power. And then, with humility, I can bring other souls closer to God.

In fact, there is a great deal of pleasure in being egoless, because then we have the sense of being a ruler or a master. God is the Almighty Authority, and so his inheritance is that his children, too, should experience His power. The sun is egoless—it continues to do its work of giving light and heat no matter what. If someone were to draw the curtains or close the windows, the sun would not stop doing its work. So, we, in the same way, have to continue doing our work. Every human being should think, "I must do my work, the things God is teaching me." Just realize what that truth is and that truth will be in your life. It can never be hidden—a diamond will sparkle even in sand or dust. So this is what we have to do: Become flawless diamonds. A diamond does not say anything for itself, so a person who has a diamond life will not need to say anything; she is incognito.

REFLECTION ON THE EGO

In silence, I give myself time and space. . . .
I know that I will experience God's love when I am able
to implement whatever it is that God asks me to do—so I
listen to God. . . .
First, God explains with love; He makes me belong to
Him and says, "You are mine; don't consider anyone else to
belong to you." God says, "Let go of the ego of the conscious-
ness, the 'I.'" I let go. . . .
I experience deep subtle love for God—and then understand
His wisdom when again He says, "Let go of the ego of the
consciousness, the 'I.'" . . .
With this deep, subtle love of God, I know how to let go of
the ego. I also let go of any awareness—any consciousness I
have—of my physical body. . . .
I know that I am a spiritual being, and that my physical
body provides the tools with which I express myself. . . .
I vow to do elevated actions and stay beyond the conscious-
ness of the arrogance of the body.

MEMORY AND THE MIND

Human beings have an amazing capacity to store memories. Our memory is so sharp that once something bad gets imprinted on it, that bad thought keeps emerging on the screen of the mind—over and over again. Even though there are dozens of good things happening in front of our eyes, nevertheless, we regurgitate, repeat and remember only those things that have been imprinted on the memory.

It is important to step back and observe our thoughts when we engage with old, painful memories. When you start observing your thoughts, you will be able to see that they are wasteful thoughts. In fact, you will also be able to see that there are more negative thoughts than wasteful thoughts. Wasteful thoughts are not useful at all. But negative thoughts are worse: They give birth to conflict inside us. Once we think negatively about someone, we start to battle with them internally. Internal battles diminish the truth deep within us, and then falsehood starts working.

Once falsehood takes over, three things start working within the mind: imagination, rumor and hearsay, and past recorded memories. Then a very subtle process starts to take place in the consciousness and all this stuff gets filed away. Inside our consciousness is the mind, the intellect—our ability to discriminate and discern what is right and wrong—and our *sanskars*—the personality traits that form our character. And so when falsehood takes over, all three things—imagination, rumor, and past negative memories—get mixed up within us.

The first, and most fundamental, lesson we teach in Raja Yoga meditation is to understand that I am a soul—I am a spiritual being. On one side then, we have the awareness of being a spiritual being, a soul, but on the other side is the awareness of being a body. One is *soul consciousness,* and the other is *body consciousness.* So we should check regularly: What am I carrying in my consciousness? When you are aware of being a body—of having body consciousness—you are thinking about your own body, bodily relationships, and possessions, the world outside, and other people's nature and personalities. This is what fills your consciousness.

In our meditation course, we teach that it is better to become soul conscious. Soul consciousness is a more elevated state to be in than body consciousness. When I really experience the subtlety of the awareness of being a soul, all the body-conscious stuff that has deeply filled my consciousness is gradually removed. When I am in the awareness of being a soul, I can experience my innate original qualities— of truth, peace, love, and happiness—and the experience of all these qualities gives me so much power that I am able to forgive and forget all the negative things recorded within me.

REFLECTION ON MEMORY AND THE MIND

Turning inward, I reflect that we all remember things that are not essential and that bring us sorrow. For a being to remember something is natural—it is automatic. . . .
But now, it is essential that I define what it is important to remember and what I don't need to think about. I need to remember only that which gives me power and not remember that which makes my energy disappear. . . .
I know that I remember people and situations that have given me sorrow again and again. Sometimes the pain is so intense that I am not even able to cry. When I remember things of sorrow and am not able to release that sorrow, then depression can follow. Today I will remember that such things are not helpful in my life.

PATIENCE

Patience brings wisdom into our lives. Patience is very important in our modern, fast-paced world. What definition comes to mind when you think of patience? In Raja Yoga, we sometimes think of patience as a state of just waiting—of just being calm. When we wait calmly, there is no emotional outburst. We are not hasty and don't carry out actions irritably.

When we are aware that we are souls—when we have soul consciousness—we are given a gate—a gate that helps us to control our feelings and emotions. Because when a person becomes impatient, a flood of thoughts and feelings emerges. We need a gate to control that flood of thoughts. Consciousness of the soul is this gate.

The moment you become aware of yourself as who you are—when you tell yourself that you are a soul, a peaceful soul—automatically the speed of your thoughts slows down. The first step to achieving patience in life is to slow down and become calm. So I need to put up the gate—by becoming soul conscious—so that thoughts and feelings stay at arm's length and become slower in speed.

To be polite is also to be patient. Being polite means allowing someone else to have what is precious to us. That way, we wait; this is being polite. Saying, "You first" is a trademark of someone who has patience. In order to have patience, I also have to be humble. Without having humility, I can't say, "You first." Patience is like sitting on a mother's lap, watching. When I am patient, I can observe myself without becoming affected by thoughts and feelings, and I can also observe others without getting affected by what they are doing—that is wisdom. Yes, to be able to watch everything yet remain detached requires patience, and that is wisdom.

In order to see everything, know everything, and yet not become a part of it—to observe, stand back, and not get affected—we need to accept and let go. If we have patience, we are able to see but not look at things, because seeing is one thing and looking is something else. Hearing and listening are also two very different things. I may hear many things, but I only listen to what I want to hear. Whatever I have listened to stays within me, but I won't remember all that I have heard. This is why when we want people to pay attention to what we are saying, we say, "Please listen." Whatever you listen to is absorbed by your intellect. It is the same with sight—we may see many things, but we only *look* at what we want to. So, there is wisdom in the patient act of seeing but not looking and hearing but not listening. When you have that wisdom—gained through being patient—you automatically use your intellect as a filter, so only that which is necessary stays with you and unnecessary things disappear.

REFLECTION ON PATIENCE

I let the body sit comfortably; I am relaxed but alert. . . .
If I am to learn patience, I must work to keep my intellect
clean and the line of my intellect clear. I know that my
intellect can only remain clean if I learn how to keep my
mind peaceful. I think of a mother who wants to clean her
home, but her child keeps crying and so she is not able to.
She has to cajole the child. . . .
So first I must keep my mind really peaceful and quiet. To
do this, I feed good thoughts to it. I let my mind rest . . . let
it be restful, not restless. . . .
I remember that my mind is my own. I mustn't let my mind
cause me distress. I cannot suppress the mind—it would
be like slapping a child. Instead, I have to give it love.
By giving my own mind love, I make it peaceful and find
patience.

HONESTY

In India, a famous religious story is remembered and often recounted: the true story of Narayan. I must have read these stories and retold them with great love many times on the path of devotion, but more importantly, I came to understand the values and truth within the stories inside myself. The story tells us of two people carrying treasures. The first man hides his treasure, saying, "Truly, I don't have anything—I have nothing," and so whatever treasures he had were lost and he was unable to move on. The other character in the tale admits, "Whatever I have I can show and reveal to you; I can tell you the truth." He retains his treasures, and is allowed to pass on. So let me make myself totally truthful. How great the contrast is between iron and gold—let me become as true as real gold.

Iron is heavy. Falsehood is like that—very heavy. Today, you also get lots of jewelry mixed with alloy. Falsehood is also like that—artificial glitter but nothing of real value. There should be nothing mixed within—in our thoughts, behavior, interaction, and relationships. Even if someone defames you, you mustn't do the same for them. No matter what anyone may say or think of you, you mustn't seek revenge. Let your thoughts instead be only pure, elevated, and filled with goodness and the intention to bring benefit to others. If there is this much truth in your own life, nobody will be able to speak lies in front of you. At every step, make sure there is honesty in your heart. If your heart is honest, God will be pleased with you. If you have courage, God will definitely help you. If your intentions are pure, then they will be fulfilled. Just keep yourself free from worry and anxiety. This is honesty.

So let your heart be completely clean like a mirror so that you are able to reflect the truth. It has been said that where there is honesty, the soul can dance. Yes, those who are honest are able to dance within. If there is falsehood within, people might look as if they are dancing, but their legs are only shaking. Where there is truth there is happiness.

REFLECTION ON FALSEHOOD

I give myself time and space. . . .
I think about honesty, truthfulness, and faithfulness. . . .
I consider my relationships—let them be faithful and honest. . . .
I think of my business relations—let me be faithful and honest. . . .
I think of my activity in the world—let there be honesty in all my interactions. . . .
Let me be number one in honesty. . . .
Let me not be dishonest with myself or with others.

SELF-RESPECT

The whole world seems to be distressed because people want to be given respect. But if you ask for respect, you can never receive it. There is only a little bit of respect in the world and a great deal more defamation. We may encounter praise, but only for a short while before we have to put up with more defamation. The world today is such that we have to deal with a lot of sorrow and only temporary happiness.

What is the key to gaining respect—and finding happiness? Honesty. Where there is honesty there will be love, and where there is love there is also respect. Honesty gives us the strength to give respect to others and to maintain our own self-respect. This equips us to tolerate defamation, disregard, and insults. We must maintain our equanimity and stability no matter what the situation may be. Whether we are facing victory or defeat, fame or defamation, praise or insults, happiness or sorrow, we must maintain our self-respect.

Often, we don't give ourselves enough time to create something of ourselves, and so we lack self-respect. As a consequence, when somebody says something to us, we immediately feel the insult of their words and get upset by them. But if we practice having an honest heart for a good amount of time, we give birth to self-respect within ourselves, and make this a continuous practice. You must give yourself enough attention to develop an elevated character.

It doesn't matter what someone else is like; you have the responsibility of giving respect to others. If someone is older than you, do not show them a stern eye. Instead, have regard for them. If you disregard elders, then how will they have love for you in their hearts? If someone is equal to you, have respect for them, too. Do not quickly retort, "Oh but this is wrong" when that person expresses an opinion; instead, have respect. With little children, inspire them by saying, "You are very good," and watch how they blossom. If we knock them down and complain and criticize them, then how will their self-respect develop?

It is up to you to be the first to give respect to your elders, your equals, and to children, too. As you do this, watch how that respect returns to you. In a nutshell, it is up to you to change yourself, reform yourself, and improve yourself so that you claim blessings from everyone—otherwise, what use is this life? We worry about others, but we don't look after ourselves. You can change this today and watch your self-respect grow.

REFLECTION ON SELF-RESPECT

For a couple of minutes, I go within. . . .
In that silence, I am not a slave—not a slave to my mind and desires, nor to the ways in which people want to move me. I don't want to be a slave. . . .
I find the seat of my self-respect, and I take that seat. . . .
When I remain in the seat of my self-respect, no one is as royal as I am. . . .
I ask myself, "Am I right in what I am doing? Do I have the power of truth within me?" . . .
I may not be perfect now, but I have the aim of becoming perfect—I will never forget that aim. . . .
Now I am able to maintain my self-respect.

SILENCE

In the old days, we would find quiet places in which to practice asking, "Who am I?" But nobody seems to have time for silence these days; their focus is not on reaching their spiritual destination. Why is silence important to a spiritual journey? In silence, we can see many things about ourselves; without silence, we just see things about ourselves that come from the external world. In silence, we talk to the self internally; we pull our own ears! This is the way to live an elevated spiritual life. I want to claim my elevated status! This is a high aim, I know, but I definitely want to reach it, and I have to start now. If we use the word *try,* it suggests that we don't really have that aim, and that we have some attachment or attraction to the body, possessions, other people, or "my" skills. Let us have this realization: I have to make the effort *now*.

To go into silence means to be introverted. In silence, everything becomes clear and we expand our consciousness. Walk in silence and your path will become clear. We have to use both feet, left and right, to reach home. We won't make it if we ask questions or say, "I'll try." When you stumble on the path, just remember the home—the benefit of that experience takes us to God.

Silence makes us forget everything, including the body. If we do not practice silence now, then when it's time to leave the body, we will be trapped in it and the soul will be left wandering around. It is wise to consider the self a soul and to remember God—indeed, it's folly not to do so—and we have to teach others to do the same. In silence, the past is not suppressed or put aside; we understand that every single scene of the drama of our past and present is unique and, whatever happens, we remain in peace. We know how to stay silent and peaceful. We know that any thought we create needs sustaining and, when sustained, will grow into something big and become difficult to quieten. So we take care not to create any distressing thoughts. In Raja Yoga, we say, "Let the creation be so beautiful that people remember the Creator through that." Each part is unique, so do your own work and stay peaceful. Then you will be able to do what God asks you; otherwise, He won't be able to use you. Go deep inside, into the Ocean, and find the jewels—don't just play with shells on the surface. Shells are natural—no one can create them—but people don't love shells. The value increases when you go deep inside, in silence, finding the jewels.

REFLECTION ON SILENCE

I go deep inside the self—I remove myself from external sounds and sights. . . .

My eyes are open and I see the scenes unfolding around me with my eyes, but I am not influenced by them. . . .

I go deeper inside—until I understand what silence is. There is only this, the experience of peace and purity . . . nothing else. . . .

The experience of silence changes into sweet silence—and then it becomes dead silence. . . .

When I go deep into that silence, it is as if I go beyond the stars, up above into a place like a tower. I have to go high up above. . . .

Up here is the One who is the highest—the One who is the Almighty, who has all powers. Then it is as if I soak up the rays of the sun and all the rubbish is incinerated. . . .

I experience the light of truth—and I feel peace, love, and power. . . .

The atmosphere here becomes very beautiful—and everything down below is able to sort itself out. . . .

I am aware of who I am and what I have to do—and I take this awareness with me.

PART 2

DADI ON
RELATIONSHIPS

TRUE LOVE

I have the great fortune to be able to serve the world. And when I travel around it, I see how thirsty people are for true love. So many people are looking for a companion who can give them true love. But what is true love?

We can all recognize something that is real, such as a real diamond. Gold is also real, but it's harder to tell whether it is real or not because we don't know how much alloy is mixed up in the gold. When you don't know how good the quality of love is, it gives rise to doubt.

True love means having honesty and truth in our hearts—not thinking "If others give me love first then I will reciprocate." Thinking "I have given so much love; what have they given me in return?" is not useful. No—the way to find true love is to learn to extend love first to yourself. When there is love for the self, there is respect for it and happiness within; then respect for everyone else will follow. First, we have to learn to cleanse our own hearts with love. Don't let any rubbish accumulate in your heart. If you do, there will be pain. By rubbish, I mean thoughts such as "This person did this to me." These only lead to blockage of the heart. Have good wishes in your mind and heart. Love will then be able to do its work.

When we think of the words *honesty* and *truth,* our attention is drawn naturally toward God and then to our own hearts. First, I ask my own heart, "What is true love?" There has to be true love. What does it mean to have true love? It means that you can share in the selfless pure love that God gives everyone. This is the love that removes sorrow and bestows happiness.

As children of God, we first take love from God. When we fill ourselves with His love, we become able to share that love with others. We are able to interact and behave with others in the right way, and so we learn what good manners are, and in that interaction, other people also experience that pure love. God tells us to take that true love and to share, being honest with everyone, because everybody is your brother and sister. From this, truth arises.

REFLECTION ON TRUE LOVE

I let the body sit comfortably; I am relaxed but alert. . . .
I go on a journey inside. . . . I remember who is giving me this knowledge and have great regard for Him. He wants us to detach from the body and to remember Him alone. . . .
I will pay attention to this. I have to learn to be and live in such a way that I don't see anything of the world, that nothing of the old world enters my intellect. . . .
If I close my eyes, some image will come into my mind. I must learn how to keep my eyes open but not to see anything. I must remember that everything I have and see now will turn to dust.
We are surrendered, so what is mine in the consciousness of being surrendered? My thoughts, my breath . . . and God. My thoughts should be so full of this true expression of love that nothing negative or wasteful comes into my mind.

FRIENDSHIP

What the world needs today is for us all to experience a loving relationship of true friendship in our everyday lives. This will inspire everyone. The truth and love that exist in our friendships are there to give other people an understanding of the meaning of life. Let me tell a tale from my own past to exemplify the importance of loving friendship. After the partition between India and Pakistan in 1947, many Hindus left Pakistan, where we were living. But for three years, we decided to stay in Pakistan, and we lived there in great safety; we experienced no difficulties at all. When we decided eventually to leave Pakistan to come to India, the local commissioner himself helped us to get onto a ship and leave for India. This is because throughout our time in Pakistan, we had behaved according to the maxim: "I am not anybody's enemy and no one is my enemy." There is so much benefit in maintaining this awareness. Say to yourself, "Let me be my own friend, make God the Supreme my friend, and also let me maintain the awareness that we are one another's friends."

The fruit of maintaining such pure feelings of friendship using the power of meditation is that you are able to serve others. I have experienced that in India, but I have also had many wonderful experiences of that ever since coming to the United Kingdom in 1974 and through my work watching Brahma Kumaris centers spring up in more than a hundred countries. Many activities have happened since then, and I see them as a fruit of all those feelings of friendship.

Truth means having *true* feelings of friendship toward others: extending good wishes and pure feelings toward other people and thinking about how to benefit them so that we share the spirit of service. Truth means not having any other feelings in our interactions with each other, only the motivation of bringing benefit.

The foundation of every relationship should be of friendship—just as when architects build buildings they start by thinking of it lasting for a long time and so take care of all the small details. In the same way, the quality of our interactions should be such that our friendships and relationships last a long time. This requires us to extend good wishes and pure feelings to everyone and to see their innate goodness. When we have such good wishes and pure feelings toward others, any weaknesses they have are removed and their goodness can emerge. True feelings of friendship really do work in this way.

In meditation, rehearse these words in your mind to harmonize your personality with others: "We are all friends; we have to work together; let me have good relationships with everybody." Then you can look at everybody and have the feeling that everyone is good. And you can listen to people with love and respect.

REFLECTION ON FRIENDSHIP

*I let the body sit comfortably; I am relaxed but alert. . . .
I go on a journey inside. I am being honest with myself. I
look into my own inner world. What are my feelings? Can
I clean out all other feelings and just simply have feelings
of good wishes and feelings of friendship? . . .*

*As I begin to do this, it feels very comfortable—very
pleasant—because in this process of cleansing, I come back
to a state of peace within myself. I am at ease with myself
and at peace with those around me . . . at peace with the
world. . . .*

*In this awareness of peace, I journey even deeper and connect
with that point of stillness at the core of my being . . . a
stillness in which there is truth mixed with nothing else—
no excuses, no reasons, but simply truth as it is. . . .*

*I begin to feel very comfortable with this experience of
peace—of truth—and I realize that these are the compo-
nents intrinsic to my original state of being. . . .*

*In my original natural state, I am peace. I am a being
of truth, and love is part of this—a love that is caring
and giving, altruistic with no other motive, except to share.*

This is who I am—a being of peace, a being of truth, a being of love. . . .

As I realize this, the power of this peace, truth, and love grows—and these qualities radiate out into this room—and out across the planet. Peace, truth, and love. . . .

I hold this awareness of who I truly am and come back to the awareness of the physical dimension and the things of here and now, but I keep this understanding of who I truly am, so that I can express it through my life, my actions, and my relationships.

FAMILY LIFE

Two intelligent people always fight. There will always be conflict between them because each thinks that he is better than the other. However, if there is one wise person and one intelligent person, there will be no conflict because a wise person understands the importance of humility and is prepared to bow before others, honoring the other person's virtues.

This is why we are told in Raja Yoga that if there are two masters in a home, there will always be quarreling. What's the solution? If one person becomes the master, the other has to become a child. If there is a master and a child in a home, one will give the orders and the other will obey them. If both people are giving orders, who is there to obey them? That leads to problems. Two heads will quarrel with each other because both want their opinion to be accepted. Wisdom means surrendering for the sake of creating unity. This is not surrendering out of weakness but out of honor.

Sometimes family members want to discuss something. Each member gives an opinion, and each one seems to be strong in opinion. So how do you decide which opinion to adopt? While giving an opinion, you are master. Fine—you don't need to suppress your opinions. We should never suppress our thinking. If you have an opinion or suggestion, speak out. Suppressing our intellect is a kind of spiritual suicide. If I suppress thoughts that come to my mind, I will not grow spiritually. So I don't need to suppress my thinking, but I also don't need to *emphasize* what I think should happen. When we offer our opinions, what do we do? We don't only give our opinions; we also want our opinions to be acted on. This is because we express them using the ego of the intellect, which thinks, "I am the best."

If I am a wise person, I give my opinion when asked, and then when the majority decides, cooperate for the sake of the majority. This is common sense. If there are ten people involved, each person's opinion cannot be acted upon. When we are wise, we find the balance between being a master and a child. When this balance is maintained, you won't have any problems because then you will get along with anyone without creating conflict. The wise person is able to interact with everyone without losing her own identity.

REFLECTION ON FAMILY LIFE

I let the body sit comfortably; I am relaxed but alert. . . .
I go on a journey inside . . . I think about how having wisdom means to have both naram *and* garam. . . .
I think first about naram, *which means humility. . . .*
I think then about garam—*this means to have the authority of truth. . . .*
Then I think about how I have both of these qualities within myself. Only when I am both naram *and* garam *can I be flexible. If I am only* garam, *I become too stiff. If I am only* naram, *then I become too fragile. . . .*
God has given me this beautiful balance—I will use it in all my relations with others.

APOLOGIZING

In the West, everyone always says, "Thank you" or "Sorry." This custom has become more common now in India, too, as an influence from the West. I understand that this is taught to people in the West from a very young age. Children are told: "You must apologize," "Say 'sorry,'" and "Say 'thank you.'"

The purpose of our lives is to live happily in honesty and truth and with love. We enter into relationships and connect with so many people in life—not just those we are related to, but with friends, friends of friends, acquaintances, and work colleagues. I understand this from my own experience.

Before I began on the spiritual path, I was connected to and in a relationship with hundreds of people, but as I embarked on the spiritual journey, I developed relationships with thousands of others. And yet throughout my whole life, I haven't spoiled a relationship with any of them.

I haven't had to apologize or say "Thank you" to people so much. It is easy for us to use these words, but let's not. Instead, let us give thanks to others from our hearts. When we use the word *forgiveness,* somehow we become heavy—it is a very heavy word. When someone is feeling pain or sorrow, he is heavy as a result of that pain or sorrow, and when you tell him to forgive the source of the problem, he becomes even heavier. When we tell somebody to forgive someone else, it is like rubbing salt on the wound. Sometimes when you tell him, "Just say sorry and forgive," he feels as if you, too, are becoming his enemy. He may then begin to blame God and ask, "What have I done to deserve to suffer in this way?" And when he cannot forgive, he keeps on experiencing more pain and sorrow, and his nature becomes hardened. Because of this, people deprive themselves of the experience of happiness, peace, and love.

Instead of urging forgiveness, it is better to sympathize with someone who has been hurt and with the person who is hurting us. This is a very subtle thing, but my experience tells me that once someone understands something, it becomes easy to implement it. When we are bankrupt of peace, love, and happiness, we experience loss. This is in fact the state of the world today, and all of you are probably experienced in this. If just one person has caused you sorrow, and as a result of that one person, you have experienced pain from ten other people, that doesn't mean that the whole world is giving out pain and sorrow. Then why is it that you become the one who relates to everybody in that negative way—why, instead, don't you become the one who shares happiness, peace, and love with others?

REFLECTION ON APOLOGIZING

When I feel heaviness and a burden inside myself, I let the body sit comfortably. . . .

I am relaxed, but alert. . . .

I go on a journey inside. . . .

I do not say "I forgive you" on a superficial level; this doesn't feel good. . . .

I say with understanding from within that whatever the other person did is okay. . . .

I maintain my love and peace and self-respect—I allow the humility and truth within me to prevent my nature from becoming hard. . . .

I let go of the hurt and heaviness—I don't allow my nature to become hard as a result of something that someone else does to me. . . .

I understand that to forgive means to forget, and I create lightness within myself.

TRANSFORMING OTHERS

If somebody is telling lies, then are you just going to keep saying this person tells lies and not trust them? No! You must be cautious, but have such a vision for the other person that you actually transform them. When the alchemist's stone comes into the company of iron, it makes the iron like itself. In the same way, you can—with your vision and attitude—transform another person. The person who is telling lies is afraid—and is acting out of fear. Lying has become a habit, and maybe that person has never had the company of someone who is honest and truthful. An honest person is brave. We need to have faith in others and give them the confidence to be honest.

This morning, I was telling someone that I have never stolen in my life; there is no trace of stealing in my past. Nobody steals in front of me, either; nobody has the courage to steal in front of me. I am not afraid of thieves. As is my attitude so is my vision. My vision helps others to change. We have to have the faith and trust in ourselves and also to have trust in others for them to be able to change. Our trust gives them strength and power. First, it gives them the power of realization, and then they are able to transform. So faith and trust are our duty.

Say, for instance, your faith or trust is broken for some reason. I might say to you, "Have trust in me. I will not do anything bad to you. I am your sister, I am your mother, and I am your friend. Just have faith in me and everything will be fine." God says the same thing to us: "Child, whatever has happened to you, forget it—put it on one side. At least have the faith that I am your Mother, your Father, and your true friend." We should at least have enough faith and trust in God to be able to reply, "Yes, you are my Mother and Father and my true friend," and the courage to act when He tells us to do something. My conscience tells me that the one who is the Father of all souls is my Father also. I have to train my intellect to have faith.

REFLECTION ON TRANSFORMING OTHERS

Sitting quietly, I reflect on what faith means to me. . . .
Is there is a reason why my faith has been broken? How can I reconnect to that faith? . . .
I reconnect—I understand that it is possible to develop faith. . . .
I can regain my faith, and then I become an example for others so that they too can learn to develop faith. . . .
I reflect that even when people give me sorrow, I am attached to them. I think about somebody who gave me sorrow in the past. She has gone, but I still remember her and experience sorrow. I know that through my faith, I can empower that person to transform. I will let this thought inspire my day.

BECOMING DETACHED

You ask me how can we practice detachment and still have our loved ones feel that we love them properly. There is no response to this because a lot of time is lost when we ask how. These are subtle things, and it's worth thinking about them further. Let us start by considering the five fingers—are they all alike? No. Now think about the right leg and the left leg. If the two were attached—used as one—would they work? Would the five fingers work if they were joined together?

According to the law of nature, to be attached means to cause loss or damage. There isn't any real use for attachment. To be in a relationship is fine—there is a husband, there is a wife, and there are children—but when there is attachment, what is the result?

I have love for everyone—I care for all of you—and I don't let go of anyone. But from childhood onward, we have to give true love. The real reason for the lack of exchange of true love is desire and attachment. There are too many desires—I want this, that, and the other—and there's too much attachment to bodily beings, possessions, and property. If we live according to desire and attachment, they influence our relationships: Somebody gives me what I desire, so I favor that person. If others don't provide me with what I want, I disregard them. If we have these habits, we transfer and instill them in others, which spoil relationships.

Attachment is subtly connected with the arrogance of the body—the ego of the body makes us concerned about what the world will say about us. Then there are three things, especially in women, that are very harmful to relationships: First, women have a lot of subtle jealousy; secondly, women have very sensitive hearts and so they feel sorrow very quickly; and thirdly, women have a lot of expectation about relationships. Because of all these concerns, we don't relate and interact with people in a helpful way. Our children learn our bad habits as they watch us. We haven't taught our children simplicity—to live a simple life—so as they grow older, they demand a great deal.

My advice is to have patience, peace, and love in your relationships—and not to be hasty in pointing the finger of blame. No, simply be peaceful, have patience, and work things out. We need to have faith and trust in ourselves, and then the courage to do the right thing. When there is honesty and love in a relationship, then that is a good relationship not based on attachment.

Human beings cannot survive and play our part in this world without relationships. So let us accept the things we receive with love. Let us satisfy people with the true love that they have not found elsewhere. They will never forget the experience of that true love. Attachment is very subtle, but when you receive such subtle love, it frees you from attachment.

REFLECTION ON DETACHMENT

First, I go into silence. . . .

Whatever has happened has accumulated in my heart, and it leads to blockages—but I say to God now relieve me of that pain. . . .

Then God says to me, "Now child, become detached because it is out of attachment that you have allowed that accumulation of sorrow." . . .

So I become so detached that I can observe that my body is here, but that you, my soul, is up above. . . .

My heart feels that this experience of detachment is so good—my heart is being healed. The pain is dispelling and peace is entering. My heart feels liberated, and then I feel as if I want to dance. . . .

When peace enters me, my face begins to smile and my problems melt away. Now there are no problems at all. . . .

I say thank you to God for liberating me from this attachment because before I was so trapped in all sorts of things. . . .

Then I say to God, "You are so detached and loving. I am going to learn that art from you so that I become detached and loving, too."

TRUST

Lots of people trust me, though in today[
world it seems to be difficult for people [
have trust in other human beings. Peop[
say that their trust has been betrayed—l[
other people, by situations, and even l[
God. The reason why many people trust n[
is not because I strive to make people tru[
me—after all, I am only a human being. [
is because my deepest desire and feeling-[
my *bhavna*—is that people should begin [
trust *themselves*. They should begin to tru[
the situations around them and also tru[
in destiny. They should begin to trust Go[
That's what I really want. It is not necessa[
for people to have trust in me as a hum[

being. When you begin to discover what it means to have trust in the self, destiny, situations, and God, then you really know the meaning of trust. Then it is not a question of you having to trust in me.

Trust is broken through misunderstandings. Someone tells me something about you, and I accept it and stop trusting you. These days what often happens is that people listen to hearsay, and this damages trust. When two people have a good relationship, there will always be a third person who will turn up to spoil that relationship with excuses or reasons. But I will never stop trusting anyone, even if you tell me that you have stopped trusting me. You might say to me, "I don't trust you anymore." Okay, so you don't have trust in me. But I will quietly and secretly—truthfully—with lots of love and good feeling, work inside myself to regain your trust. I will never say, "I have tried so much with this person, there must be some unfinished karma or unfinished business—I'll leave it." I would never say that our relationship or friendship has to end now. That would be cowardice.

If I have made a mistake or somebody else has made a mistake, let me be so strong and so sensible that I don't allow my trust to shatter, even if somebody else has made a mistake. I have to be able to forgive his mistake. If he loses trust in me and I lose trust in him, then you start seeing everybody else in that same way. Then you gradually lose trust in many people and you don't have trust left in anyone. That kind of life is not a life of happiness. The habit of losing trust becomes a *sanskara*, or personality trait, of mistrust, which then makes me disheartened and unhappy. I should never lose my trust in anyone or give up hope on anyone by losing trust in him.

If you lose trust in someone today, you will start remembering all the things that have gone wrong in the past, and you will see how your lack of trust in someone is justified on the basis of past actions. It is as if you have given up on the value of trust. We mustn't allow this to happen. I won't allow it to happen. I will make you recognize the value of trust through my good wishes and the pure feeling that emanates from my true heart. It might take time, but I work tirelessly to help you with love from my heart. Because trust is the light of our lives. There is no life without trust. Once I lose my trust in myself or others, then I lose trust in God, as well.

REFLECTION ON TRUST

Turning inward, I find myself. . . .
I recognize myself inside—it may take time for other people to recognize me, but at least I recognize myself. . . .
I see what you are inside. Whatever it is that you need inside, I want to be able to give you that, with love, so that you are able to recognize your own self inside. . . .
The reason why you trust me is because I don't see you using these outer eyes—I see you from my heart—and that is why you like it. . . .
God sees my heart and that is why I like God looking at me. God doesn't see me as human beings would see me.

PASSING JUDGMENT

When we pass judgment on others, we waste our energy. Acting like a lawyer means taking sides. And then, of course, we want one side to have victory and the other defeat. So I do not allow my mind to play the game of the lawyer. It is a bad business.

But if you want to be a judge, be a true judge who has accurate balance, by becoming an accurate judge of your own life. Examine what was happening in the past that wasn't right—when you can see that accurately, you will be able to see your weaknesses. This makes you a very sensible judge and allows you to erase the past and keep the present good. You will not have any fear or anxiety about the future. You won't spend time worrying whether maybe the same thing will happen again.

Three virtues help us move on from the urge to judge. If you cultivate these, even when others judge you, your heart will remain strong. And if others try to shake you, you will be unshakeable. These virtues are patience, contentment, and tolerance. When you are patient and content, you are an emperor—you experience no desires or pulls. Tolerance makes us sensible. If we lack tolerance, we hold onto things from the past and feel the pain that comes with them. We also view others with the same vision and spread that pain. If somebody has judged you, you will hold it in your memory, and your behavior with them will be influenced by your memories. You can't give comfort to anyone from your heart because there are other feelings there. So you have to be able to make your heart strong, and to be able to understand what is happening in the hearts of others. To do this, first forgive yourself; have love and compassion in your heart. Without them, you will be unable to look after yourself.

Once you are able to take care of yourself, then you can be an instrument to help look after others by understanding the reasons for their pain. If our own hearts are clean, we understand ourselves, and if our own hearts are honest, we have power.

REFLECTION ON PASSING JUDGMENT

First, I go into silence. . . .
If I remember the things of the past—this is what I had, this is what happened—there is pain. . . .
But these things are not here now, so why should I remember them? There is new life now—an awakening is happening in my soul. . . .
Now I know myself, I recognize myself, I understand myself—so what more do I want?. . . .
I know that I am no longer dependent on anyone. And so what if I wasn't clean? Now I can clean myself—yes, I know that my soul is pure. I feel peaceful—and this peace also heals the self. . . .
When I feel peaceful, I love myself, and wisdom develops. . . .
Now I am powerful and there is no weakness. So everything is okay—everything is right.

SEEKING FORGIVENESS

Today it has become very hard for people to ask for forgiveness—they say to themselves, "Why should I ask for forgiveness? *I* am not going to ask for forgiveness." That is the strength of the ego! The arrogance within us makes it really hard for us to ask for forgiveness. It somehow seems easy to remember the things that have gone wrong, but to ask for forgiveness is a different matter.

If you get into the mode of remembering something that someone has done to you, it also becomes a habit to snub or ignore that person if they then cross your path. For instance, if you share an office with a colleague and develop that state of mind, you might try to avoid the other person by waiting until he has gone before entering the room. When you are unable to forgive and forget, you also can't work with that person and will keep on complaining and finding faults with the little things he does wrong. The other person might have lots of good aspects—and others even may try to point them out—but we protest by picking up on the things that he has done wrong.

We need to learn to let go in such a way that we are able to forget totally about the incident that happened in the past—so that it is as if it never happened, and then the other person is able to forget, too. So if something happens in the morning, by the evening it is gone and there is again love between the two parties. We need to create an atmosphere of love so that we can see soul to soul—see who we both really are. Then there is no need for anyone to ask forgiveness: We forget things in such a way and to such an extent that the other person forgets them, too. To achieve this, create a feeling inside you as if you are consoling the other person in your mind and comforting the other person's heart, saying, "It is okay—the conflict is over."

When we take time to go into silence and understand, our consciousness goes to a higher level and we begin to think in a completely different way. We start to have feelings of mercy and compassion, feelings of wanting to help people rather than feelings that are contrary, of not forgetting and forgiving. When I was little, I remembered one line from my religious text—the line was "Mercy is the seed of religion, and ego is the mother of sin." Those who have feelings of mercy are able to receive blessings. The one who has a merciful nature is also very loving. When I have such maturity, I am able to be full of love—I can see the specialty of another person and encourage that specialty to come out even more.

When I do not have the feelings of forgiveness and mercy, when I speak to correct someone, my tone of voice will indicate this—it will be harsh; people will feel corrected and they won't like it. If my intentions and feelings are right, then even if I don't use words, people will pick up those good feelings from me and will correct things by themselves.

REFLECTION ON SEEKING FORGIVENESS

To forgive is a matter of just one second. . . .
I go inside—in silence, I look inside myself. . . .
Forgiveness means first of all forgiving myself—I forgive
my own self and I ask God to forgive me, as well. . . .
I remember that I am a child of God—I let my mind go
upward to God—and then the power that comes from Him
helps me to forget everything. . . .

I make a pact with myself—that I am not going to remember
the wrong things I have done and all the wrong things that
others have done to me. . . .
I remain peaceful and pure deep within. When I have that
kind of feeling toward myself, God is able to give me the
wisdom to be able to make it happen. . . .
When that flow of love comes from God, I feel all the vio-
lence and falsehood inside me is dissolving—and then that
helps to dissolve the falsehood in the world. . . .
In silence, I focus on having a good relationship, connec-
tion, and communication with God and with everybody.
We are all each other's friends and God is our friend.

PART 3

DADI ON WORK

THE BIG THINGS AND
THE SMALL THINGS

How can you make the environment and the people you work with happier and more positive? By doing your job appropriately. *What is your job? To keep things in proportion.* Say, for instance, there is a fire. Are you going to ask the questions, "Why is the fire burning? How come there is a fire?" No, your job in this situation is simply to fetch a bucket of water and put that fire out. Even if there is only a small spark of fire, your job is not to fan the flames so that the fire increases—your job is to cool down the fire. That means if something happens, your job is to change the atmosphere and create a mood of positivity.

The reason why I have managed not to spoil my relationships with anyone is because I have understood this. I say to myself, "Let me not make small things big, but if big things are happening, let me be able to make those big things small." This is your job, too. If we let ourselves become weak, ordinary, and powerless, then our hearts won't be big enough to give happiness to others. If you have a tendency not to see your own mistakes or if you think you are always the one at fault and feel bad and guilty about your actions, you will be unable to build that atmosphere of positivity.

To remedy this—to maintain a sense of proportion—when you do something wrong, learn to forgive yourself. Ask for forgiveness from God, and also learn to forgive others. When we remind other people of their mistakes, they feel bad about it, so it is important to make others forget their mistakes, too, through your interactions with them. This is the way to keep the small things small, and make the big things smaller, too. This is the way to build a positive atmosphere at work and at home.

REFLECTION ON THE BIG THINGS AND THE SMALL THINGS

*In order to bring everything into perspective, I have to pre-
pare my mind. . . .*

*I must understand and allow myself to experience the orig-
inal nature of my soul—which is peace. I will let myself be
quiet and peaceful. . . .*

*God is teaching me how to make my own mind my best
friend by making it peaceful. Only then can He sit in my
mind. Until now my mind has been very mischievous. To
end that mischievousness, I have to learn to think about
spiritual things . . . and to make myself peaceful. In soul
consciousness, my mind is attracted to God . . . gets to
know Him and falls in love. My intellect can then link
to God. . . .*

*When I really get to know Him, then I become "lost in
God." There is no more beautiful experience than this.
God has a great deal of attraction, and I allow that
attraction to pull my soul. Then everything else falls into
perspective . . . and small things seem unimportant.*

HOPE AND EXPECTATION

There is a difference between having hopes
and having expectations. Some English
words—such as *hope* and *expectation*—are
complicated and so they create complications in your life. When you have hopes in
someone, your hopes are filled with love and
patience and you have *bhavna*, good feelings.

Expectation is different. It causes the
breakdown of that love and patience, those
good feelings, and harms our interaction with
others. If I have expectations of you and you
have expectations of me, there will always be
the feeling between us that you don't understand me and don't know what I want and
I don't know what you want. This cannot

nurture transformation. When there is expectation, there isn't a depth and spirituality in our relationship with each other because we both feel that we don't *understand* each other.

There are many people whom I know and have worked with for many years. I have had to change and adjust myself so that I don't have expectations of them. I maintain good feelings of hope and respect, and I understand that whatever needs to happen will happen one day. This is an inner thing. It means constantly maintaining honesty, truth, and love in our relationships with colleagues. If we have this aim, then we should never forget this aim. We must never let go of honesty and love.

Look inside yourself and see the value of the goodness that is inside you; then look at the value of the goodness in others. Don't let your ego get mixed up in goodness—don't insult others even if they make a little mistake or do not value their own goodness when carrying out tasks. This is not being sensible at all. When there is any sorrow or discomfort and no pleasure in exchanging or cooperating in interactions with others, then what is the meaning of life? To continue to experience happiness, we must have hopeful relationships filled with honesty and love.

REFLECTION ON HOPE

In silence, I give myself time and space. . . .

I think about how when I have experiences and become experienced, others also gain experiences through me. Then my experiences can bring others hope. Spiritual understanding is such that it leads me into experiences and I will then want to share those hopes and expectations with others. I will be able to help people to deal with challenges emotionally and able to bring them consolation. . . .

So today I must keep the awareness not only that God is watching me but also that the world is watching me. This awareness will help me to make my life good, and spread my hope to others.

MAKING DECISIONS

No task can be accomplished alone. We require the cooperation of other people in our everyday tasks, and it becomes necessary to accept each other's ideas. But what if some of those ideas don't feel right in your heart?

I listen to everybody's ideas with deep respect when I have to make a difficult decision, and I should listen to them because they are all my companions in service. I listen to them and say, "Yes, what you are saying is true, but what about this? Do you also think that this is a good idea?" I do not disagree with others instantly and cut down their ideas, saying "That is not right." Even my face does not show them that I don't agree with them.

In order to make the right decision, I have to make my intellect very deep, very subtle, and very broad all at the same time. Some people judge things on the basis of their past experiences—they mix their past with the present, thinking "Well, this happened in the past, so this is how we should think at the present time, too." My conscience tells me that I mustn't mix the past with the present. We should think, "I have *learned* from my past, it is useful to me now, and so this is the way I should think in the future." There was a reason for me not to be successful in the past, but now I am able to make it possible for me to be successful.

When we instill in ourselves the habit of going into silence and developing this wisdom, then, day by day, we start to come up with ideas in such a way that others say, "What you said was the right thing."

REFLECTION ON MAKING DECISIONS

It is good to put everything else aside and sit in remembrance. There is great enjoyment in remembrance. In fact, it is the time to become free . . . to be able to get totally absorbed. If I do everything God says, I will automatically be happy—and always make the right decision. We have to make our minds and bodies cool. For this, hourly traffic control is very important. Once an hour, let your mind become silent and let your body be cool. . . .

When the soul belongs completely to God, then the body becomes cool. Yogis are the ones with cool bodies; without any type of agitation, there is peace and coolness in both mind and body. There should be such a quietness of the body that there is no agitation. The senses then work with coolness and peace—and every decision will be the right one.

LIVING IN THE PRESENT

The most important thing is to pay attention to the present moment and make it positive, despite what has happened in the past. If you keep the past alive in the present by thinking, "That shouldn't have happened" or "It would have been better that way," then your future won't be good.

Having trust in the universe—or whatever you might like to call it—means trusting that whatever has happened until now is fine. It is finished, and it is the best thing that could have occurred. You can't change what has happened now. Having trust in the universe means making your present well-intended—and not worrying about the future. If your present is right, it is guaranteed that your future will be right, too. This is very deep wisdom.

My experience tells me that the past can even be transformed if my present moment is right. So even if I made a mistake yesterday or committed a sin this morning, I need now to do such acts of charity—perform such elevated actions—that I make others forget the mistakes I made. If you do good, positive, and well-intended actions now, others will forget the wrong deeds you did this morning. Say, for instance, you got angry with me half an hour ago. Now, half an hour later, I smile as if nothing has happened—I am not reminding you that you got angry. If I do remind you, then I spoil my present. Because then you will react again, saying, "Why did you do that?" And I will say, "You did do that, didn't you?" That is wrong. My future is spoilt. To have trust in the universal drama makes us more sensible.

If you keep looking back at your past, you will keep experiencing pain. You will be upset and unhappy, and cry. When I think about what happened in the past, I cry. It doesn't matter whose fault it was; don't feel guilty, because this makes you cry. Don't be angry with someone because she doesn't realize her guilt; this will spoil your relationship with her. Then nobody will be your friend. So it is important to recognize that time and people are your friends. Become your own friend, too, to make your future good.

REFLECTION ON LIVING IN THE PRESENT

In silence, I give myself time and space. . . .
Right now I say to myself, "Whatever has happened has happened. So even if I think about it being wrong, it won't change." . . .
I know if I dwell on the past it will make the present feel bad, too. It will stop me from having the zeal and enthusiasm to do good things today. . . .
Now I know that yesterday has passed, this morning has passed. It's finished. . . .
Whatever has happened is good, and whatever is going to happen is good. . . .
The present moment is in my hand—so is the future. . . .
I know the past cannot come back into my life.

SUCCESS IN BUSINESS

To have trust in the business world doesn't mean you will end up penniless. To have trust means to be sensible. To trust does not mean allowing somebody to cut my pocket and take all my money. Trust means that I have such truth within me that nobody can cheat me or deceive me.

My father was a businessman. Brahma Baba, the founder of Brahma Kumaris, was also a businessman. He was a jeweler, and even if he had just one customer, he would do such good business with him that he could spend the rest of his time in spiritual endeavors. A customer would have so much trust in him that he wouldn't go anywhere else.

If I myself am a cheat, it is very easy for people to cheat me. If I am truthful and honest and I have integrity, then people will not cheat me. In fact, they will be willing to pay me more. They won't even bargain! My relationship with everyone should be full of honesty and the truth that I can be successful in business. My business must be based upon honesty and integrity. Truth and honesty make me sensible. If someone is preparing to cheat and deceive us, we get vibrations from him that he is about to cheat us. We have to remain cautious and alert. We live in a world of deception, but if I allow myself to enter into deception and then regret, that is my weakness.

So if we are truthful, and honest, then our trust becomes our power. Trust is such a power that it won't allow us to become weak. Instead, it gives power and strength to those who are weak. They see your trust, and they start to recognize the power and value of trust.

When you pay full attention to whatever duty you have been given, you are able to become successful. Our duties—and the only work we have to do—are to become peaceful and give peace to others. You don't have to do anything else. When there is peace, love, and happiness, then there is power within you. If there isn't peace, there cannot be love. In order to become peaceful, you definitely need patience. If there is the slightest bit of impatience, you will lose peace and love and your face will change. Then others will take sorrow from the words that you speak.

REFLECTION ON SUCCESS IN BUSINESS

Turning inward, I find myself. . . .

Faith and enthusiasm will make me fly. I must keep the faith that I will be victorious. But for this, I have to stop looking outside—stop seeing and listening to external things. Instead, I will turn inward, listen to God, and move forward. . . .

If I keep seeing and listening to outside things, I will create many doubts within myself. I will learn not to look at, think about, or question what others are doing. . . .

Now I make the choice to leave behind such things that make my soul diseased and move toward total spiritual health and victory. By having true faith, I will receive the reward. I will feel that God is helping me in everything— in every aspect of my life. . . .

Now I will make my stage so high that whatever happens externally I will remain—then no circumstances will be able to shake me.

REAL INTELLIGENCE

Many people in the world are intelligent, clever, and smart—we cannot compete with them in terms of intelligence and smartness. But very few people in the world are wise and sensible. We don't become intelligent by studying Raja Yoga—we become sensible and wise. When God adopts us as His children, He gives us wisdom as our inheritance. We gain that wisdom when we practice yoga of the intellect by connecting with Him.

It is important to understand how God transfers His wisdom to us when we become His children. In our previous lives, we all had an intellect and some kind of intelligence; what we lacked was wisdom. For example, we knew what patience and tolerance were, but couldn't use them in our lives when it was necessary.

What God did, first of all, was to give us knowledge of the soul. By doing this, He made our intellect divine. The intellect was spiritualized when it received this knowledge. Then truth—the conscience that was sleeping—was awakened. When the conscience awakens to soul consciousness, we see everything from a different angle.

So first we grew in wisdom by gaining an awareness of who we are. Once our conscience is awakened, our intellect develops the power of precise *discrimination.* Then we are able to discern, discriminate, and judge things properly. One definition of wisdom is having the necessary power of discrimination and judgment to lead a life of balance. Before, when we lacked awareness of our true selves, there was imbalance. I was partial in my judgment and discrimination—I couldn't see things from both angles. So we gained the wisdom to see right and wrong, the eye of wisdom that discriminates truth from falsehood and equips us to pick the right course of action. Our vision broadened, too—to have wisdom means to have *far-sightedness.*

When someone is very narrow-minded, he is not regarded as wise. Someone who has wisdom always looks at things with a broad mind and far-reaching sight—in an unlimited way. That is why he is able to accept things as they are. The sign of a wise person is someone who is able to accept himself and others as they are, and so he doesn't put demands on anyone. That is why it is always good to be in the company of wise people: You are at ease and feel relaxed.

This third eye of wisdom gives us a feeling of understanding, consideration, and concern for others. That is what it means to be wise. When somebody is intelligent, they can be selfish, wanting everything for themselves. The wise always have a feeling of understanding and consideration for others. This consideration enables a wise person to accommodate and tolerate. Wisdom helps us to discriminate, so we pause before doing something—with the feeling of concern for others. For the sake of keeping others happy, the wise are willing to sacrifice anything of their own.

Wisdom means not just being beyond confusion, but also to have *clarity*. Because there is such clarity in what we do, there is no confusion or upheaval— what you do is clearly set out in front of you. Wisdom means being able to understand lessons learned from the past, to use experiences from the past to correct your present and brighten your future.

REFLECTION ON REAL INTELLIGENCE

I let the body sit comfortably; I am relaxed but alert. . . .
I am wise; I do not dwell in the past—I do not ignore the past—I do not live in the future. I am far-sighted, but at the same time I enjoy the present. . . .
I have attention, not tension—that is wisdom. . . .
I will think of the consequences of each word I speak. . . .
With each action I perform, I will consider the effect on others. I will think before I act. . . .
I am far-sighted and without fear of the future. . . .
I can use the present in a worthwhile way.

STABILITY

From today let go of your worries! The one who worries is always in a hurry and will sometimes speak hastily with bitterness—so go make a curry! Worriers waste time thinking too much. They may worry about money or other things— perhaps they worry that the work they do is not very accurate. Despite the amount of work there is to do, when we trust in our intellect— trusting that everything will be fine—we can be stable. To remain stable, you need to have good feelings and trust in the self and in others. You also need a great deal of faith in the intellect, faith in the self, and faith in God. When you have faith that the work you are doing is of benefit to others, the intellect doesn't shake.

So fix your mind on a task that is good and your mind will become peaceful. If we worry, we cannot create good thoughts, so let us maintain pure and positive thoughts. The mind can then be peaceful and the intellect stable. Things may disturb you, but by keeping your intellect stable, you will be unshakeable. When you have good feelings, trust, and faith, you will be able to take the right course of action. Cleaning out the heart and making the intellect stable is the first step. A clean heart is an honest heart. If you look in the mirror of your heart and clean that mirror, you will see your true self. When there is truth in the heart, the mind accepts what the heart says. Think of the mind as a baby. Pacify the baby with a great deal of love. Sing it a lullaby and put it to sleep. This is such magic; the mind becomes so peaceful when we do this.

To remain stable, a chair needs four legs of equal length. We must make ourselves strong with four things: *knowledge, yoga (meditation), application of knowledge in our lives,* and *service.* Knowledge means understanding, yoga means connection with God, and then there needs to be attention on the self to create a good character by removing all defects and seeing virtues in everyone. We also need to serve others with honesty. If you have these four things, you will be stable and able to shower peace on others. To be stable is our honor—if we shake and others see us shaking, that is dishonor.

There are four more things we need: *honesty, love, cooperation,* and *the ability to be good company.* When we practice these accurately, there is stability. Then you feel happy, your relationships become good, and nobody else needs to worry about you. Today is the day to end the illness of worry. Let patience be your doctor. No worry, no problems, no doubts!

REFLECTION ON STABILITY

As I begin to know myself, I begin to develop faith in myself. . . .
I know who I am—I am a child of God. . . .
I have faith in myself, faith in God, and faith in my human family. . . .
The entire human family is my brothers and sisters—when I

have this awareness, I feel that each scene of the drama is going to be of benefit and is going to be filled with goodness. . . .

God is my parent—I need have no fear, no need for worry; I simply have to deepen this connection with my Mother and my Father. . . .

As I hold God's hand and follow the directions God gives, I feel the canopy of protection above me. The canopy is imperishable—the canopy is with me at all times. As I work in the direction He has shown, the canopy of blessings stays with me. . . .

Faith in myself means that I recognize the original greatness of the self in my original state of being. . . .

There is purity—there is love—there is truth. As I discover these within myself, I see these in all my sisters and my brothers.

I keep this divine connection so that God's support is able to surround me and protect me. . . .

The chaos and upheaval of the world increases, but God's protection keeps me safe—safe today—safe tomorrow— safe forever. . . .

I remain stable in this awareness of God's company and companionship.

STRENGTH

Today, tiredness is a type of sickness. Nowadays, whether young or old, people are tired. Those who don't know how to cooperate with others will get tired. When there is no love, there is tiredness. When we work with honesty and love, everything happens without tiredness. It is not a matter of how long we sleep. Tiredness is created by wasteful and negative thoughts and actions. Positive thoughts and noble actions give strength, a strength that includes energy and power. When someone is weak, he needs strength. A punctured tire is without strength: weak and useless. If there is no strength, there is tiredness. The solution is to pay attention to creating elevated thoughts and performing noble actions. By understanding this spiritual knowledge, you can end your weaknesses and become powerful and strong. You will then be able to do a lot of good work without getting tired.

Those who work for money count the hours and the salary. If such workers think they are not receiving enough salary, they leave. Working for love, I can work for sixteen hours a day with happiness and without ever getting tired. Doing service brings energy. Don't allow the self to have wasteful thoughts. End such weakness! If someone is insulted when doing a task, their reaction will cause feelings of weakness and tiredness. If we experience this, then we won't want to do the work or will do it half-heartedly. If we do the work with honesty— as best we can—we do not take sorrow from insult but receive the fruit of instant happiness. Then we feel the happiness accumulating and such happiness brings strength.

With love, too, comes a great deal of happiness that can build strength. If we share our positive inner feelings with others—our good wishes and feelings of purity of heart—everyone benefits. Just think of the effect if all of us were to create pure feelings for ourselves and for one another. What strength we would accumulate! To create these pure feelings, you need to stop looking outside the self and criticizing—which causes negativity to collect inside the self so that we become tired and weak.

Strength comes from using our time in a worthwhile way and by creating positive thoughts. So give your time with happiness. Pay attention to having good intentions and elevated feelings and to speaking sweet words. First, create noble thoughts. By having good intentions, a good attitude, and a good vision of others, you will be able to speak words that inspire others. As a result, you will be able to create a spiritual income for yourself through your noble actions.

REFLECTION ON STRENGTH

In the awareness of being, I connect with the Almighty, the
Source of light and love and might. . . .
From the Almighty, I am filled with strength—this divine
strength enables me to have pure, positive thoughts—
thoughts of truth—thoughts of the eternal self. . . .
I am that being of light. I am eternal and immortal,
beyond space and beyond time—beyond the influences of the
world of matter. . . .
I am light and might—and as I stay connected with the
Almighty, I am filled with God's power—the power of
peace. . . .
Peace pervades the soul—peace then radiates out into the
world, and that peace establishes a natural state of peace
around me.

PART 4

❋

DADI ON HEALING
THE WORLD

DIFFERENT FAITHS

We may have faith in religion, but there are innumerable religions. There is only one God. There is not a different god for every religion. You may say, "I am a Christian" or "I am a Hindu," but God doesn't say you are Christian or Hindu. Whether someone is Hindu or Christian or Muslim, God has love for us all.

It is a mistake to think there are different gods, and because of this mistake, we have stumbled and become distant from one another. We should all realize our mistake from deep within and understand that all of us belong to one God, and therefore all of us are one. You may point out the differences in belief between Hindus, Christians, and Muslims, but why do we quarrel within our own family? We have the habit of battling within our families, within our countries, and in the world. And who would say that they don't quarrel with themselves in their mind? We have to stop all this internal and external fighting and make ourselves peaceful—we are not on this planet to fight, but to be honest, peaceful, and open to the light.

It is very easy to stop the fighting. We just need to keep the intellect clean and the line of intellect—our connection with God—clear. When we all think and talk about righteous things, the atmosphere changes, even in the space of half an hour. If every day we gave ourselves food for thought, for one hour we could change so much.

It is a big mistake to not give ourselves that time to sit, make ourselves peaceful, and take love from God. We also don't devote enough quality time to interacting peacefully with each other. Instead, we are caught up in racing around doing things. We think, talk, and do our work in a hurried way. We are always rushing!

My experience is that God has love for each and every single human being. He sees the condition of the world; He sees that there is so much sorrow and so many difficulties. He sees us rushing around creating a bad atmosphere and bad relations with each other. He wants us to stop this. When I say God, I mean the only God, the one God. Often when people refer to God—whether Christians, Muslims, or Hindus—their fingers naturally point upward and they say, "That One, up above." He is the one who belongs to everybody.

REFLECTION ON DIFFERENT FAITHS

I let the body sit comfortably; I am relaxed but alert. . . .
God is the Father of all souls, and yet He says to me per-
sonally, "You are my child. Come to me." Then the internal
feeling of "belonging" comes. . . .
Christ had the awareness of being the child of God and so
was able to become the messenger of God. So let me now give
myself the time and space to think about these things and
to establish such a relationship with God that I can really
know what He wants from me in this life. . . .
In India, God is known as the Mother as well as the
Father, so let me think of God as a mother who will care
for and take care of me for my whole life. Then I feel that
God is saying to me, "Oh my sweet, sweet child." . . .
Now I take myself into absolute silence . . . the quality
of silence where there is only awareness of me and the
Supreme.

THE CONDITION OF
YOUNG PEOPLE

I have great concern for our children, the conditions they live in, and what the state of childhood has become. Wherever we live around the world, there are cases of our young people using drugs, stealing money to feed their habit, and getting in trouble with the police. But the fact is in this day and age parents often don't give their children the kind of sustenance they need to ensure their welfare and well-being. They give birth to children, but they don't know how to take care of those children. As the children grow up, they see their parents engaged in a frivolous lifestyle of decorating themselves and entertaining themselves. People in the world are very lazy and careless, too. At the time that they should be awake they are asleep, and at the time they should be sleeping they are awake. They prefer to stay awake until late at night, and then in the early hours of the morning, when it is time to arise, they want to sleep! These are bad habits, so what habits will the children learn, what company will they have? Another factor in their behavior is the source of their listening. We become like the things we hear, but instead of listening to good things, children often listen to the news and they become like the things they hear.

I traveled to Mexico recently, and people there were asking me to talk to the youth and tell them not to take drugs. I said, "First, call the parents and the teachers." I wanted to talk to them before I spoke to the children. Because when children get good sustenance and good company, this keeps them safe from the harmful things of the world. Children also learn to feel safe inside themselves, and this translates into a feeling of safety in the world. We need especially to be in good company because the kinds of habits people form are the direct result of the company they keep.

So, in order to bring up our children, we first need to have self-control and self-discipline ourselves. If you learn to discipline yourself, then you will be able to teach your children this skill. If you don't do this, then how will your children learn? Whatever has happened has happened, okay? Whatever mistakes children have made have been made. But now, in order to keep them with you and in your care, forgive them and enable them to remain close to you by showing them your love and making sure they don't spend time in bad company.

REFLECTION ON THE CONDITION OF YOUNG PEOPLE

First, I go into silence. . . .

Let my own conduct be such that my children learn from me. . . .

Is it because they don't receive true love that they are drawn to bad habits? But even if my children are in bad company or have bad habits, I must not let it cause me sorrow or worry—or how can I help them? . . .

Instead, I offer them my support and care by sending them good wishes and having pure feelings for them. . . .

My love, forgiveness, and mercy will help them. . . .

I create a peaceful atmosphere and send them those peaceful vibrations. . . .

Their souls will receive my vibrations of peace and that will help.

PRACTICAL PEACE

People of the world ask how we can make the world a better place, how can we reform it? The reality is that I have to reform myself first—only then will the world change. We see the world, but the world also sees us. Today, the people of the world should see those who are not fighting and quarreling with others. We should shine the light on those who spend their lives giving out love and cooperating with others and the world.

It has been thirty years now since I have been in England. The conditions of the world have worsened over those thirty years, but on the other hand, there has also been change for the better. Between the first ten years of my time there and the second and third decades, I noticed that people changed a great deal. Previously, it had been difficult to gather together even ten people to talk about spiritual matters. Now people have much more interest in the spiritual life and many people have accepted it. As a result, many people's lives have changed for the better. This is what the world needs. People want and need to see those experiencing practical peace in their everyday lives.

We listen to the global news, but what can we do about all that fighting and tragedy? Let us become the ones who give peace and love back to the world— by doing that, we help the world. Millions and millions of people are fighting and quarreling, but some hundred thousands of us, at least, should become the ones who restore peace in the world. These are the kind of people who are needed in the world today. During times of darkness, one lamp is not sufficient; we need lamps all over the place. When one light is lit, then many other flames can be lit from it.

We also have to want to learn from one another— whether we live in the East or the West. We have to have good *bhavna*—good feelings—so that we become the bridge that brings two ways of life together. What are the differences we need to bridge? In the East, people have a great deal of devotional feeling. In their hearts, there is love for God and love for spirituality, but also they have good feelings toward each other and lovely manners. In the West, the intellect is used a lot, and because of this, there is a lack of love and honesty. The relationship between people has become very tenuous, leading to difficulties such as loneliness. But the truth is that the West has influenced the East.

In the West, we need to have stronger feelings of respect for one another and stronger feelings of obedience to the elderly. We need to generate feelings of love for one another and share more with each other. From a very young age until old age, we have to learn to care for each other. Everybody needs care.

People are realizing this in the West now, and as the ancient way of life of the East is coming to the West, so East and West are becoming one. We are all human beings; deep down inside, we are the same, with the same basic needs. We must use our vision, our intellect, and our hearts to make the world a more positive place.

REFLECTION ON PRACTICAL PEACE

I sit with myself and I speak to myself. . . .

I cannot afford to waste time waiting for the world to change and become a better place. I have to initiate the change individually and personally. . . .

I say to myself, "I need to change—I need to reform." Once I take that step of transformation, I will watch my family begin to change, my community begin to change, and my country begin to change—and then the world will also change. . . .

But I need a lot of patience to do this. . . .

First, I need to be patient with myself—I must not scold myself when I cannot see myself changing. No, let me have mercy for myself—and then with patience talk to myself and interact with others with love. I will be patient, be merciful, be forgiving, be loving, be honest with myself—I will change. . . .

God will help me to change. . . .

When I create such feelings of mercy and forgiveness by talking to myself, then when I interact with others, I will have the same feelings for them—everything is going to be okay. . . .

I don't ask, "How can I do it? How can I move forward?" I just get on with it. I march forward and take everybody with me. . . .

It will be so easy to bring about transformation. . . . We just do it!

ON SUPERFICIALITY

In the world today, love is based on the superficial form and external wealth. There is love for those who have wealth—but where there isn't wealth, there is no love. If someone is healthy, strong, and able to move with splendor and power, then, yes, people love them. But there is no love for someone who is simple and ordinary. This is in such contrast to the love we are able to experience from God. This love liberates us from a love that causes sorrow or leads to deception.

When I was young, people's perception of me was that I was short with a big face. I was neither beautiful nor educated. But I told myself that it didn't matter what people thought of me. I didn't want to wear makeup and have different hairstyles to make myself look beautiful on the surface. *I had love for God and God loved me—so it didn't matter what people thought of me.*

Often people only see what is on the surface. If a woman is wearing makeup, a nice dress, and expensive jewelry, and has made an effort in her appearance, then she is liked by other people and gets noticed. But if a woman is quiet, kind, and does not give anyone sorrow, she is not seen as being good; to the contrary, she is often seen as having no value and is not easily noticed by other people.

In order to develop love and trust for yourself, you should not love artificial things or desire the kind of superficial respect that is shown just to please you. What you need is your real self-worth. Whatever you are, whoever you are, this is what you are and you belong to God. I felt that from my childhood, but after gaining some spiritual understanding, it became my nature. So no matter how much someone insults me or defames me now, I will never let go of my self-respect or become affected by them. If I were drawn to anything artificial, I wouldn't be able to hold firmly to my self-respect. Artificiality causes fluctuations in self-respect, and if we fluctuate, we can't trust ourselves. I don't want people to relate to me on a superficial level—whether they are impressed by my profession, home, car, appearance, or money. I don't see other people with that vision, and I don't want others to see me in that way.

I have been on this spiritual journey for seventy years of my life, and because of the experience of God's love, I have never felt the pull of anything materialistic or of human beings in that limited way. My experience has been so rich.

REFLECTION ON SUPERFICIALITY

I let the body sit comfortably; I am relaxed but alert. . . .
I go on a journey inside. . . .
I consider myself to be fortunate—I appreciate what I have. . . .
I do not compare myself with others—I do not compete with others. I am happy with what I have. . . .
I think, "Yes, I am fortunate"—and then the more I think that, the more I start to watch that fortune increase. . . .
When I have no doubt in my own self, the power of faith and confidence in my own self grows. . . .
I do not see anyone's position—or wealth—or age—or any other factor at all. . . .
I simply see the child—the soul—the child of God.

COMPETITION AND ADVERSE COMMENTS

Here, in the West, people become particularly isolated, and in that state of isolation, they think too much. Because of that, there is a lack of clarity in their communication with others. Communication becomes very superficial—and because of this, the heart fails to really open up so that people can relate at a deeper level.

Instead, in today's world, it is more common for people to come into competition with each other, to comment about each other, and to correct each other. Because of this, some people lose their sense of self-worth and self-respect. They are unable to build themselves back up again.

So let us not come into competition, compare, comment, or correct. And if somebody else chooses to do these things to us, let us not allow them to make us unhappy. There was a woman I knew who had the habit of correcting everyone. No matter what others did, it was never good enough to please her. So others felt unhappy that no matter what they did, they were never able to make her feel satisfied. When we see such behavior, we have to learn not to engage in that behavior ourselves. Instead, let us do everything with attention and accuracy and with so much love that nobody needs to make any comment at all about what we do. And if they say something anyway, let's not keep it in our minds. Let us help those people to remove that problem. This is an incognito act of charity.

REFLECTION ON COMPETITION AND
ADVERSE COMMENTS

In silence, I give myself time and space. . . .

If there is something lacking within me—a virtue or a quality or a power—let me correct myself. Then I will maintain my self-respect. . . .

If I do have negativity or a weakness within me and somebody is telling me about it, let me not feel sorrow or get upset about it. Instead, let me accept it and change it. . . .

The ones who defame me are my friends, because they have drawn my attention to something about me so that I can correct myself. . . .

I do not let such words or actions upset me or dishearten me . . . but inside quietly, I endeavor to change so that the weaknesses become a thing of the past.

HOARDING POSSESSIONS

People have the habit of holding on to old things—they might have lots of new things, but somehow they still hang on to all the old things, as well; they never want to part with those old possessions. Sometime those items are not even of any use—they may have broken or stopped working. But still we won't throw them away or donate them to charity! If the possessions we were hoarding were good things, that would be a different matter, but we seem to be hoarding the bad things! Why on earth are we holding on to these old things that are of no use to us?

Meditation is a way of clearing out all the rubbish we accumulate within us. It means not listening to things that are not good and not looking at the things that are not beneficial. When we do this, we don't store up bad things. In meditation, we learn the art of listening to and seeing what we need to hear and see, and not listening to or seeing the things we don't need to hear or see. In the meditation that we teach in Raja Yoga, we don't close our eyes. They are open, but they are being used in the right way. They are still and they are focused—not distractedly looking here and there.

I am not suggesting that we don't see or hear what is going on. All I am saying is don't see and hear things that are not good—don't go into the difficult details and start hoarding them away inside.

When we start seeing, hearing, and hoarding bad things, it gives birth to three things: fear, anxiety or worry, and sorrow. But when we transform our way of seeing, hearing, and speaking by making sure that we see only good things and hear only good things, then we must make sure that we fully register them and take them in. This gives birth to courage, truth, and faith.

REFLECTION ON POSSESSIONS

For a couple of minutes, I go within. . . .
In that silence, I free myself from thinking about good or
bad, likes or dislikes. . . .
My head becomes really calm and cool. . . .
My heart becomes happy, light, and full of joy. . . .
My nature and the way I interact with other people become
very sweet. . . .
I smile and I keep smiling . . . because there are no more
inner complaints or criticisms. . . .
How did I achieve all that? . . .
I just paid simple attention—I did not repeat wrong or
bad or old things. . . .
I threw out all the rubbish from inside me and made enough
inner space that I can experience and express the goodness
within me.

WORLD UNITY

Over the years, I have noticed that human beings are human beings—it doesn't matter which country they are from; we all have a similar nature. We all have two eyes, two ears, a nose, and a mouth—is there anything different between people in Africa, America, or England? No; we all have the same eyes, ears, nose, and mouth, and the same feet and hands. Sometimes we don't understand another person's language, but from their body language and gestures, we understand what kind of mood they are in. And when any one of us gets angry, it is the same, as well. When we suffer from attachment, it is the same; greed also is consistent; ego and arrogance are the same—it is the same for everybody.

We are able to go beyond the limits of color, race, and culture—and even beyond the differences of nature and personality. Love and honesty help us to belong to one another and bring us into unity. We are one; we are one family, and we are brought together with one motivation: to serve. This awareness of unity brings so much joy. There is so much joy and happiness in unity. When there is unity, a mountain can be lifted.

On my own I can belong to God, and on my own I can also have the motivation to serve, but when it comes to serving our huge world, there is so much suffering that what can I do on my own? When it comes to the subject of service, God tells us that we all have to come together and serve in unity. When there are good feelings of love, trust, and faith through understanding God, then we can come together and create a powerful gathering that is able to serve.

Let us think of the example of the honey bee. The honey bee does the work by itself, but only when the bees are together can honey be produced. When flies sit on dirt and rubbish, they spread germs and illnesses. When bees sit on flowers, they gather pollen and create honey together, and that can heal infection and prevent illnesses. Those who pick up rubbish can never come into the garden of unity.

We should follow the example of the honey bee, and attempt to take goodness from everyone, and see the virtues in all. Then, when we come together seeing the specialties and the goodness of each other, there can be unity and strength. Unity means to be able to see virtues, absorb virtues, and donate virtues. We can call this happy family a gathering but also a huge army. It is a huge spiritual army that is able to uplift the world! In the army, we have to be ever-ready and present to do whatever service is necessary. Not alone but all together, serving together.

When there is unity, there are no problems. There is great happiness, joy, and love in unity. But when there is quarreling, people say there must be some fault on both sides—one hand cannot create a quarrel. The quarrel arrives when both hands come together. When we clap our hands together, it can be with great joy and happiness. Both hands can come together with humility and respect, too, as a gesture of honor or prayer. But two hands can also come together in conflict—I must never allow that to happen.

It is everyone's desire that heaven should come on earth. Heaven isn't up above; we have to create it here on earth. Through our character and behavior, we *can* create heaven here. Out of multimillions, a few will emerge who want to do this. What is the population of the world now? God says that even nine hundred thousand is enough to create heaven. If nine hundred thousand are ready to change, this world could become heaven very soon. Then there will be victory for truth and non-violence. Sins will be conquered, truth will return, and we will be able to treat each other with love and happiness. Between the earth and the sky, all human beings are actually one family, all children of God. *When God sees that there is a gathering of unity— a group that comes together with love—He says, "I will be present in your midst also."* This is my experience.

REFLECTION ON WORLD UNITY

I gather with others with one desire—the motivation that God has served me and I have benefited, so now let everyone benefit also so that the world serves God. . . .

When that motivation is present in all of us, then God is present with us. . . .

No one of you is mine—and yet all of you are mine. We are one family, traveling to one home—we are all children of the one Father. . . .

The world has become divided; hearts have been broken into pieces. Each heart has been broken into many pieces. The world is also in pieces now—and so now we will put it together with love and with truth. . . .

Let I—the soul—individually make such a deep effort and such a full effort—not just a little effort but a full effort—that I am truly able to make God belong to me.

STEALING AND DONATING

Whether you steal or give in donation, you use the same hand. When stealing, you use the hand to take, and when donating, you open the same hand to give. So, in stealing something, we are taking something and making it ours, but in giving, we are sharing.

What is the impact of these different acts on the heart? When we give, the heart believes that nobody needs to know about it, and if we steal, the heart hopes that nobody will see what we are doing. If a police car passes by and stops outside, there is a fear that the police have come for us. And out of fear, our legs start trembling. So why do we perform bad, wrong, or unmindful actions if it causes fear? In Sindhi, there is an expression that translates as: "The one who is honest and truthful always dances." This is an automatic response because those who are honest have no fear—they therefore never have to question what will happen or how things will occur. They just have the faith that whatever will happen is very good and so do not worry. They dance instead.

The whole world needs to give now. Each one of us should understand that the responsibility lies in our own hands. We shouldn't think that if someone else starts I will follow. It is up to me to start acting generously now and to continue doing it for others to see—then they will automatically start giving, too. We should continue giving and give so much that we lose count of our good deeds. To do charitable work is such a great action that when we do it, we can do no wrong. Others will follow our example, creating a gathering of charitable souls engaged in good work. Then, from whichever country we are from, in that country the wave of charity will spread.

The world will witness the example of countries that are doing this much good. Is this possible? Of course!

REFLECTION ON STEALING AND DONATING

I give myself time and space. . . .
Whatever someone else is taking, let me do the work of repairing and putting it right. . . .
Until the point of death, my work is to learn—and to keep bowing down. Those who have the desire to gain something keep their heads raised high—but I bow my head a little and then others can respect and garland me. . . .
The best decoration is the garland of virtues—flowers made with the thread of truth. . . .
I see the virtues of humility, respect in everyone. . . .
We come together—each one of us—with all our virtues so that we can garland the world with the garland of virtues.

ON DYING

At the time of dying or leaving the body, we have to let go of everything. From the point of birth until the point of death, all we have done is just grab at everything, wanting everything to belong to us. At the moment of death, our hands will open up—we won't be able to take anything with us—we should think about this in life. In fact, we've wasted years of our lives in chasing after things, in wanting things. So we should ask ourselves this question: "What have I done?" Whether at the end you are taken to a graveyard and buried or to a crematorium and cremated, the people who live on after you ask the same question: "What did that person do in his life?"

What are temples, churches, and mosques built for? Whose monuments are these? They are the monuments of the great souls and memorials to them because those people have been incarnations of truth and humility. And because of these two qualities—truth and humility—all over the world, these monuments are their memorials. So we have to ask ourselves this question: "What will be my memorial?"

I saw with my own eyes the qualities of perfect truth and humility in the founder of Brahma Kumaris, Brahma Baba. He was the embodiment of these qualities; he was the incarnation of them. There was no trace of falsehood in his life. Even though he engaged his life in such an elevated way, he never ever said, "I did this" or "I am the one who has to do that." He always said that God was the one doing everything. And if we ever praised him, he would not listen. He would always say, "Praise the One who is the Almighty, the One up above." We would say, "We have seen you doing these things." And he would say, "No, no, no, not at all—it's not me. It is God who is inspiring and doing everything." We never heard

Baba praise himself, and he would never listen to any praise that we gave him. He would always say, "Children, praise that One." He would stand children in front of him and say that it was the children who deserved praise. These teachings helped me a great deal in my life.

REFLECTION ON DYING

I go inward in silence. . . .
I let there be peace and love within myself—and I realize that my protector and my teacher is God himself—and I understand that He is mine! . . .
And so whatever is His wealth and His virtue is also my property. . . .
And that wealth is imperishable—and it will go with me even when I leave this body. . . .
Even while I, the soul, am in this body, that wealth of virtues will do its work and do service.

PART 5

GETTING TO
KNOW GOD

GOD'S LOVE

What is love? L.O.V.E. L is for the life that love creates, O is for zero, V is for victory, and E is for ever. I have experienced many adverse situations in my life and overcome them with love. Love is so powerful that it can resolve all problems. Even if a difficult situation arises, it will not be able to over-power the love. Instead, the love will over-power the problem. How can I help you, too, to remove your fear or guilt and find love?

Let's start helping you by asking what there is to be afraid of or guilty about? When you have a connection with the Almighty, there is no longer any fear or guilt. Secondly, let's ask how you can live in such a way that you never feel guilt or fear. It's easy: Simply live with all humans and all animals with love. Never have any dislike or hatred for anyone, and never be impressed by anyone either, because if we are impressed, we will, at some point, be deceived.

Ask yourself this: "What or who do I love? Do I love the body, money, or status?" Love these and there will be fear. We cannot prevent the body from growing old. Money and status can disappear overnight through no fault of our own. But when we have real love and honesty in our relationships, there is no fear and we arrive at a position of security, from which we have the power to end all negativity.

There are three forms of love: *true love, affection,* and *friendship.* Affection and friendship can sometimes become dependency, and then, inevitably, love becomes selfish because it needs constant reassurance from another. If I am dependent on the love of any human beings or I make somebody else dependent on me, then that love is false. There can be deception, too, in any type of relationship, whether it be between mother and child, husband and wife, or between friends. In fact, this is why there is so much sorrow in the world today. True love is without dependency, without deception, without selfishness, and without fluctuation. What is true love? Spiritual love is true love. It is not based on anything physical. Spiritual love (agape) is the deep bond of affection that never breaks and that brings us together in harmony.

DADI
JANKI

REFLECTION ON GOD'S LOVE

Sitting quietly, I reflect on matters of the heart. When I am looking outside seeing people and objects, then desires, attachments, and fears come to me. . . .

But when I look within, I arrive at a point of stillness inside. . . .

I become aware of that which is sacred, and I become aware of the presence of the Divine. . . .

From the source of love, I am filled with pure, unconditional love—love that empowers me—love that uplifts me—love that awakens the purity and divinity within me. . . .

In the presence of God's pure love, there is no fear and no worry. God's love fills me with strength. . . . God's love removes the darkness of fear. . . .

And the love of the Ocean of Love reaches out and encompasses the entire planet. Each and every human soul, every one of the animal souls, each aspect of nature is embraced by this love. . . .

God's love creates the world, chasing away all fear and all worry. I hold this love in my heart and create a world of love.

HAVING A RELATIONSHIP
WITH GOD

In today's world, people's trust in God is broken—and there are many people who don't even want to trust in God. They ask, "What's the need?" This is something we should devote time to thinking about.

There comes a moment in all our lives when we begin to see that there is no support for us from any direction. Difficult situations make us ask, finally and ultimately, "Who is my support?" The intellect starts to think and to understand that nobody can be the truth the way God can be the truth.

At this time, we may ask the question, "God, who are you and what are you like?"

We may ask this question so that we can take real peace from God and experience that peace and love and happiness in our lives. *When human beings want real peace and love, then their attention is drawn in the direction of God because they know that they are not going to get them from anywhere else.*

Previously, I too used to think, "How can I possibly forge a relationship with God?" Then I thought about how to make an electric connection between two wires: All you have to do is remove the plastic rubber from between the wires; then they can be connected. In the same way, we have to remove that rubber from ourselves. What is that rubber? We have to remove from our own consciousness and mind an awareness of ourselves as a limited physical being. Then other things that have filled the soul— such as guilt or fear—will be cleaned out. As I made the connection with God, who is a spiritual entity just like I am, then I started to experience His love, peace, purity, and bliss in my own life. Previously, I had only heard praise of God—I didn't really know that He was full of all these qualities.

My soul had lost these qualities, and I had been asking for love from human beings like a beggar. Now I don't want anything. God gives me real love. How did this happen? First, desire was created in the intellect. The desire started to become more intense, and then I didn't want anything else—I just wanted to get to know God more deeply. Then my connection was forged with God. I began to understand that I, the soul, am separate from my body and I am loved by God. It was wonderful to recognize my true self at last. When I recognized God as that truth, I was able to gain that recognition of my own inner self.

Once this has happened, the soul begins to accept from the heart the feeling that God the Supreme is my Mother, my Father, my friend, my guide, my teacher, and also my guru. I play with those different relationships now as I would an instrument. I have that much inner support from God. I have to recognize Him with my intellect, accept Him from my heart, and know Him from my experience. The feeling is one of regaining what I had lost. I am able to appreciate God and say to Him, "You have given back to me what I had lost."

REFLECTION ON HAVING A
RELATIONSHIP WITH GOD

*I go inside myself—I become introverted. I allow my
thoughts to become stable and concentrated. . . .
I feel an intense desire to get to know God—I say, "I want
to know you and recognize you." With this deep desire,
I let my intellect become free from ordinary things—from
everyday thoughts and from the distractions of the past. . . .
Then my inner eye opens. . . . I recognize God, and then all
my confusion vanishes and my intellect stops wondering.
I begin to love peace—I become light and I receive might
from God.*

WHO IS GOD?

Even though I am in my nineties, I still consider myself to be a child of God, filled with the power of His love. First of all, I consider God to be my *Mother.* I have the feeling that God is my True Mother because a mother always has an acceptance of the child. She says, "Whatever you are like, you are mine." This is what God says to me.

God is also my *Father.* As my Mother, God embraces me and takes me in her arms. As the Father, He also indicates to me to become a person of authority. When somebody is adopted by someone of great authority, he becomes very happy—no matter what he was like before—because now he belongs to someone of high status.

God is also my *teacher*. In the form of the teacher, God shows me how to have a life of virtue. God has taught me with so much love and with such language that those words can never be forgotten.

God is also my *friend* and *companion*. He gives me good company. He is a wonderful friend. This friendship is made easy because of love. When there are two friends, they have equality. God the Almighty Authority is my friend and is making me like Himself.

He is also my *Satguru*, my Supreme Guide. He guides me and I obey. Through my relationship with God, I am able to experience so much love from Him and develop even more love for Him.

These relationships, connections, and communication with God can help to remove sorrow from the world and suffering in relationships. The Father is a very sweet, loving Father—he has a lot of love for us—and so he says, "You have been searching, and now it is time for you to move forward." He helps not through one relationship but all relationships.

As a Mother, God accepts us exactly as we are. God doesn't see the color, the nationality, the background, the poverty or the wealth—none of these things. No one in the world can accept us without checking these things first, but He doesn't check in any way. He just says, "Come to me. Come into the light." God stands with His arms wide open, saying, "Come to me." This is how beloved He is. And so he accepts us in the form of the Mother.

And then the Mother says, "Look at your Father and see who your Father is." And so our eyes open and we ask, "Who is my Father and what does he want of me?" As I watch my Father, I see all His virtues. When I see the virtues, I say, "I want all those virtues in my life—but I don't have the power." And God says, "Connect with me, and I will give you the power." He is the truth; He is the Almighty. No one else has the truth as He does, and truth is a very big virtue to have. I need power to be able to have truth in my life, and He says, "Have a connection with me, and I will give you the power."

As a teacher, God continues to explain over and over again with love and patience. As a friend, he says, "Keep your heart light. Whatever comes into your heart, tell me and I will help you." He helps a great deal as a friend.

Make God your friend, and you will see the wonders of His love and company. Make Him your companion so that he can give you His company. A parent cannot give that much company. When a child grows up, she needs a companion. God says, "I will be your companion and take you to your destination. I won't let go of you halfway." And so the heart says, "I want to stay with Him, be with Him, eat with Him, and I want to go home with Him." There is no other concern. And then whatever is happening is good, and whatever will happen will be good. There is nothing to worry about.

As you imbibe the nourishment of happiness and become strong, you can give others the benefit of your company. You have received the One whose love is giving, and you have looked after it, so your life can give light to others. The light draws near, and God says, "Move forward one step, and I will help you to move eight steps forward." I was very far away. He was the Highest on High, and I had fallen to the lowest, but with love, I was able to move forward, and so the One above came close to me. And so with my courage and true heart and His help, He became mine.

REFLECTION ON WHO IS GOD?

I let the body sit comfortably; I am relaxed but alert. . . .
I go on a journey inside. . . .
I think of God as my Mother. She has a great deal of love for
me. She says, "Come, my royal child—the light of my eyes."
With so much love, I feel so light and so worthy. . . .
I think of God as my Father—his virtues and power
transform me from an ordinary human being so that my
divine qualities emerge. . . .
I think of God as my friend and I say, "I can't do this,"
and He says, "Come, I will give you my company," and He
becomes my friend. Perhaps I am not able to speak openly
with my Mother and Father, but I can speak of the things
of the heart to my friend. . . .
I think of God as my teacher and my true guru, Satguru.
He gives me good advice and counsel to save me from fol-
lowing the wrong track. . . .
Then He says to me, "Whatever thought you have, if you
have it with a true heart, then it will become real." I feel
the wonder of first recognizing Him and then celebrating
this meeting with Him.

DRAWING CLOSER TO GOD

First, God teaches us how to take His love and make use of His love. But the more we use His love, the more our understanding grows and the more we are able to increase our love. Then the experience of that love works like a power. The power that comes from love enables us to experience success. When we experience success in our lives by feeling God's love, then we achieve a pure feeling—*bhavna*—and know that the same experience should be available for everyone on earth.

I remember a very beautiful scene: One day in Mount Abu in our small hall, which we refer to as a History Hall, I saw the founder of Brahma Kumaris, Brahma Baba, dancing all by himself. I was absolutely amazed! Just look at him, I thought, he is so light on his feet, because he has so much love for himself and because he has received so many blessings from other people. From that day, I promised myself that I would also be the same—so light because I love my own self. So secretly I love myself! God makes us so worthy, so let us have love for God and also for ourselves.

You might be very busy people, and you probably claim that you don't have enough time to love yourself! But you have to make time to love yourself. Do bear in mind, however, that it is not so easy to love yourself just like that! We have to do something to qualify to have love for our own selves. When you qualify, then God will give you love and then you will receive love from everyone.

In my devotional days, I used to read the scriptures, and in the *Bhagavad Gita* there is a conversation between Arjuna and Krishna. We remember Arjuna because he was able to implement everything God said to him. I used to talk with God, saying that I, too, wanted to become like Arjuna. I wanted to be able to implement everything God says in my life. I also wanted to become a lover of God. Gopis—the lovers of God—don't feel jealous when others also have love for God. They simply have a lot of love for God as well as a lot of love for themselves. When God is among us, then we all have love for each other.

REFLECTION ON DRAWING CLOSER TO GOD

In silence, I give myself time and space. . . .
I have to become the student. I am a true child of God; therefore, I am a true student of God the Teacher. . . .
God himself is my teacher, and He is telling me what I have to do. If I am naughty and mischievous, what good can his teachings do for me? . . .
So I say, "God, you are my teacher. I want to follow what you are teaching me. Make me good; then others will learn from my example." . . .
To make a decision takes a miniscule part of one second, and after I have made the decision, I realize that this is my choice and I carry it through—and then I see results. . . .

REFLECTION ON DRAWING CLOSER TO GOD *continued*

*I ask questions such as "What is the purpose of my life? Do
I want to live according to the world's expectations? Should
I be something on the external level, even though I am something else internally? Is this the way I want to be?" . . .
I say, "God, I am your child. If I am to live in this world,
let my life be such that I am of use to you." I can choose
what I want to do. . . . I will be honest—the truth cannot
be hidden. . . .
The One above says to me, "Child, the unity between your
faith and trust in me leads to wonder."*

DADI
JANKI

166

RESTORING OUR CONNECTION

When we use the third eye, we see what we cannot see through our physical eyes. That is why we are said to have a "far-reaching intellect." My divine intellect works like a TV. With a TV, you can see scenes happening thousands of miles away as if they were very close. It also brings events that happened five thousand years ago close to our intellect, as though they took place a minute ago. When everything is this clear, we don't have to ask, "Why is this happening?" We know things are repeating.

So why might your vision not be so clear? There must be something wrong in the connection. When the television picture is not clear, there's often something wrong in the environment—perhaps with the weather or a loose connection. Maybe the plug is not fully in the socket or the wires are loose. If your intellect is filled with wasteful thoughts, you will find there is disturbance. Just like disturbance in the weather.

So to improve our vision, we have to correct those problems, making sure that the connection is well-established. A superficial connection acts like a loose contact: There may be light on the screen, but no picture when the connection is not firm. In the same way, we have to make sure that our connection with Baba is secure in all our relationships. Think of an electric lead. Even though the wire looks like one entity, inside there are many small wires fused together. So, we must connect all our relationships with the one God and then "plug" in. My connection is well-formed; I have no wasteful thoughts—and this is why images of what happened five thousand years ago seem very clear to me.

We have to experiment with our connection so that we get the same thought and carry out the same action as we did five thousand years ago. Then time is not wasted. Sometimes we are successful in making a good connection; at other times we are not that accurate—if the intellect is not clear, we won't get the right connection. For that, *we have to allow God to work through us.* We have to allow our intellect to be connected to God in all our relationships, because then our intellect becomes divine and our conscience is awakened.

The power of realization becomes deeper as we practice this form of connection, or yoga. That is why it is important—however much time we sit—to really make sure that the yoga of our intellect is connected accurately with God, so that we really feel that His qualities and powers are coming through to us. We might think of ourselves as like a battery being charged. This charge cleanses the intellect, too. When the intellect is clear, it becomes easy to understand others and easy to understand ourselves.

Yoga practice allows us to gain this wisdom, which comes in the form of blessings from God and manifests in the form of virtues and powers in our everyday lives. This is why after practicing meditation for some time, you will find that your patience or tolerance or the nature of your humility has improved. You may not even notice it, but other people do. It is due to the practice of meditation. The more we meditate, the more those qualities enter into our practical lives.

So try to spend a longer time in meditation. Because to allow a battery to remain charged, you have to connect it to the generator for a long period. Three or five minutes will warm it up, but not top up the energy. To get the energy really flowing, you need to be connected to God for at least half an hour each day.

REFLECTION ON RESTORING OUR CONNECTION

For thirty minutes, I just sit—I meditate. . . .
I experience the Almighty as the Ocean of Love. The power
of God's love claims my heart and allows me to let go of
the past—I am able to forgive and forget so that I have
nothing but good feelings and good wishes. . . .
I am the Source of all energy—I enjoy what it means to
experience all the values and virtues I am being charged
with. It is like bathing in the rays of the sun and drawing
in energy. . . .
That energy is the power to transform. . . .
That energy changes me, the soul. That energy changes the
atmosphere and makes it pure again. That energy restores
a golden age, the age of truth. . . .
In that moment, the moment of God's power—God's light
and God's might—God's energy and love transform the
world, and the world returns to a state of harmony.

DIVINE INSTRUCTION

When I begin to know myself, God gives a signal: "Look at me and see who I am. See me and then see yourself. See yourself detached from the body and detached from bodily beings." And by seeing myself, my inner eye opens and I am able to see God. When I have the desire to know Him, then I am able to see Him and recognize Him.

When God speaks to us, our vision is drawn upward, and God says, "You are mine." There is a contract between us based on the fact that I belong to Him and He belongs to me. And so a deep relationship is forged between the imperishable Supreme and me, the imperishable soul. As I forge that relationship, I discover that God is my Mother, my Father, my beloved, my friend, my companion, and my true guru. God is all relationships—the essence of all.

Then God gives us another signal: that we must recognize that our bodies—indeed, the whole world—is perishable. There is wonder in His words as he says, "Hey soul, recognize that all of this is perishable. Understand this well. But you, the soul, are imperishable, and I, your Father, am also imperishable, and all the treasures that you can receive from me will stay with you eternally. Purity, peace, happiness, love—let all of this stay with you. Child, did you receive this?" He asks the soul. If we have received it, we should look after it. The Father gives us an inheritance, but only if the child has the wisdom to look after it.

He also tells us to forget the things that we have heard so far. Forget all the information that you have studied. When you forget those things, then you listen well to what He has to say and you will study the things He has to teach you instead of focusing on worldly knowledge. It is a law of the universe that if you love someone, then you will enjoy listening to her, and you will experience a deep feeling of faith that whatever God is saying is for your benefit. We call that *divine instruction*—the instructions of God. He gives us very good instruction on how to make the intellect divine and elevated. So let us not follow the dictates of our own desires and our own minds. Let us be careful so that our old nature and habits do not get mixed up with our divine intellect. Instead, let us maintain the awakening that shows us our true selves and let us keep the clean, happy mind that we have once all the dirt has been removed. Then the mind will adhere to discipline without any difficulty—tell it to be quiet and it becomes so—and when there is a need to think, the mind thinks in the right way. It doesn't think too much, and so it is always able to rest. God has taught us so much. He is the teacher—and those who are sensible accept instructions from a teacher. He is also the guru, the guide, pointing out to us the right direction to move in. When a child is young, his parents hold his hand and guide the child. When he is a little older, they watch, checking whether he is going in the right direction. So when God says that you are not a little child anymore—you are older now and have the wisdom to move in the right direction—still He watches over you and looks after you. Sometimes He is ahead to clear the path. Sometimes He is behind to keep watch. And so there is never any doubt whether you will be able to move forward or not. He is always making you move in the right way.

REFLECTION ON DIVINE INSTRUCTION

I sit in silence—I respond to the magnetic pull of love. . . .
I find myself surrounded by the unconditional love of the
Supreme Mother—God's love embraces me and surrounds
me, as I am, exactly, with no conditions, with no judg-
ments. . . . And this light of love cleanses my soul. . . .
As I am cleansed, I discover my Father, the being of truth,
the Almighty Authority. The love of the Mother prepares me
to recognize the being of truth—and in the presence of truth,
I see the truth hidden within my own inner being. . . .
God's power fills me with strength so that I can throw
away my illusions, my limitations, and my falsehood—
and the truth within me begins to shine. . . .
The light of love and the light of truth transform me—the
child of the Creator reflects the qualities of the Creator and
the gifts of the Supreme. The inheritance of the Supreme
stays with me. . . .
Purity, love, peace, joy, and truth—I hold them in my
being and share them through my life.

KNOWING THE SUPREME

Wisdom is firstly to know the soul you are and secondly to know the *Supreme Soul*. Without knowing these two, there is confusion. It is as if the soul is in darkness. When I am with the Supreme, I can stay light and can draw might to myself. If there is something right, let me do it. If I feel something isn't right, let me leave it. When there is confusion, there is darkness. When there is light, everything becomes clear.

When someone does something good, ego can manifest itself. On the other hand, someone may want to hide something he has done wrong, which is also a sign of ego. The power of silence puts an end to the ego. Silence creates humility and patience; it teaches us to understand what will happen and to know when we should just wait and see. If we fill our heads with the news of other people and the world, instead of having humility and patience, we will ask, "How, what, and why?" To ask "How?" and "Why?" is a waste of time. Remain in silence, and see how the confusion is automatically removed. When we learn to understand ourselves in silence and when we connect with God in silence, then we will know what we have to do. By focusing on silence, we become aware of the presence of God. This silence is powerful and carries a loving presence. It is an alive and loving silence.

By keeping this connection with God, we can feel tranquil and secure and any confusion will be vanquished. When we are confused, it is difficult to have faith either in ourselves or in anyone else. Wisdom emerges when confusion ends. Wisdom says, "Don't think too much; conserve your energy. Thoughts that are unnecessary like 'How?' and 'Why?' are a waste of energy." By going deeply into silence, your own wisdom will become divine and you will become more aware of yourself as a spiritual being.

The mind then becomes peaceful, and the intellect is freed to work clearly and accurately. It has an understanding of what is right and wrong, good and bad, true and false. This is what it means to use the power of spiritual understanding—wisdom—and of connection with God—yoga. Karma yoga means keeping a connection with God while engaging in action. The word *karma* means action, while *yoga* denotes connection and relationship. As a result of practicing this combination, you will more easily notice and understand your negative actions and find the power to stop performing them. It will be clearer to you what type of actions you should and shouldn't perform. Neither will you stimulate the ego either by the achievement of a great deal or the hopelessness of having failed in what you set out to do.

How do you relate to the world now that you have this relationship with God—and how does the world relate to you? Acknowledge that no one except God can be the truth, and recognize that every human being can know this for himself. The Supreme Soul is truth. God has love for every soul, whether someone is a sinner or a saint or a devotee of God.

REFLECTION ON KNOWING THE SUPREME

*Going inward in silence, I understand who I truly am. . . .
I, the eternal being, am the child of the Supreme. And in
this eternal connection of love, God blesses me with the gift of
wisdom—wisdom to understand myself very deeply, wisdom to
recognize the Divine, and wisdom to know what I must do. . . .
Deep in this connection with the Supreme, there is God's
light—the light of wisdom—the light of truth. . . .
God's light removes the darkness from the intellect and I can
see. Now I can see the path—I can see the destination . . .
and I hold the hand of the One who can guide me to the
destination of liberation and perfection. . . .
God's blessings of truth equip me to realize that my own
original state is a state of perfection. . . .
As is the Creator, so is the creation: the Creator—the
Absolute—the pure One—the perfect One. . . .
With the blessings of God's truth, I recognize that I, the
child of God, am a reflection of the Creator. . . .
I had forgotten my own state of perfection, and now God
reminds me. . . .*

As the memory awakens—as wisdom unfolds—darkness is
banished and perfection emerges and begins to shine. . . .
The light of truth teaches not only me, the soul, but the
light of truth transforms the world. . . .
Together, we move into the world of light, the world of
truth.

About the Brahma Kumaris
World Spiritual University
http://www.kbwsu.org

International Headquarters
P.O. Box No. 2
Mount Abu 307501
Rajasthan, India
Tel: (+91) 2974-38261 to 68
Fax: (+91) 2974-38952
Email: abu@bkindia.com

**International Coordinating Office and
Regional Office for Europe and the Middle East**
Global Cooperation House
65–69 Pound Lane
London NW10 NHH, UK
Tel (+44) 208-727-3350
Fax: (+44) 208-727-3351
Email: London@bkws.org

Regional Offices
Africa
Global Museum for a Better World
Maua Close, off Parklands Road, Westlands
P.O. Box 123, Sarit Center
Nairobi, Kenya
Tel: (+254) 20-374-3572
Fax: (+254) 20-374-2885

Email:nairobi@bkwsu.org

Australia and Southeast Asia
78 Alt Street
Sydney, NSW 2131, Australia
Tel: (+61) 2-9716-7066
Fax: (+61) 2-9716-7795
Email: ashfield@au.bkwsu.org

The Americas and the Caribbean
Global Harmony House
46 S. Middle Neck Road
Great Neck, NY 11021, USA
Tel: (+1) 516-773-0971
Fax: (+1) 516-773-0976
Email:newyork@bkwsu.org

Russia, CIS, and the Baltic Countries
2 Gospitalnaya Ploschad, Building 1
Moscow, 111020, Russia
Tel: (+7) 499-263-02-47
Fax: (+7) 499-261-32-24
Email: Moscow@bkwsu.org
Brahma Kumaris Publications
www.bkpublications.com
enquiries@bkpublications.com

ABOUT THE AUTHOR

Dadi Janki is a founding member of the Brahma Kumaris World Spiritual University and is its administrative head, having spent more than seventy years of her life expanding the organization internationally. She is a pioneer of the modern form of the ancient art of Raja Yoga. Through this structured and disciplined method of spiritual development, she has shown thousands of people of all backgrounds and walks of life how to regain true self-respect, become free of addictive and negative tendencies, and thereby be able to contribute more to present-day society as well as a future world. In 1992, Dadi was invited to be one of the ten Keepers of Wisdom, an eminent group of world spiritual leaders convened to advise the Earth Summit in Brazil on the fundamental spiritual dilemmas that underpin current worldwide environment issues. In 2004, she was awarded the Medal of Independence by the king of Jordan for humanitarian work. She is an international patron of Rights and Humanity, a patron of the World Congress of Faiths, and a member of the Global Peace Initiative of Women.